ALIVE *in the* SPIRIT

GENE L. JEFFRIES, TH.D.

A PRACTICAL, BIBLICAL INSIGHT INTO
THE PERSON AND THE WORK OF THE HOLY SPIRIT

Alive in the Spirit
By Gene L. Jeffries

© Copyright 1995, 2005, 2012. Gene L. Jeffries.
All Rights Reserved.

No part of this book may be reproduced in any form without permission in writing from the author, except in the case of brief quotations embodied in critical articles or reviews.

Unless otherwise noted, all Scripture quotations in this book are from the New American Standard Bible, Copyright 1960, 1962, 1963, 1968, 1971, 1972, 1973, 1975, 1977, 1979, 1981, 1983, 1985, 1987, 1989, 1991 by the Lockman Foundation, and are used with permission.

Some Scripture quotations taken from the King James Version and American Standard Version of the Bible.

ISBN: 978-1-935986-30-0

Lynchburg, Va.
www.liberty.edu/libertyuniversitypress

PUBLISHER'S ACKNOWLEDGMENTS

A special thank you to all the individuals who assisted in the creation of this publication:

PROOFREADER: Kirstin Spivey

EDITORIAL ASSISTANT: Arielle Bielicki

PROJECT EDITOR: Steven Guest

EDITORIAL MANAGER: Sarah Funderburke

LAYOUT AND GRAPHICS: Rachel Dugan

PREFACE

When Ronald Reagan was President of the United States, he called attention to this generation as the "information generation." Individuals with personal computers, he said, had access to more information than many of the nation's leaders had until only a few years ago.

The craving for information is not limited to the secular world. It is the thirst of the Christian Church as well. We may well wonder what Solomon had in mind when he warned that "the writing of many books is endless..." (Ecclesiastes 12:12a).

Could he possibly have envisioned the plethora of volumes that now flood our world market? How many books actually existed in Solomon's day, anyway? Apparently enough, because he also noted that the "excessive devotion to books is wearying to the body" (Ecclesiastes 12:12b), (remarkably similar to statements made by many college students today!).

Yet, when the dust has settled upon the immensity of available information, there is still no guarantee that the information will translate into anything meaningful. It's not how much information one has, it's how much *grasp* one has on the information.

ALIVE IN THE SPIRIT

When the late Dr. Earl O. Harding was serving as the Executive Secretary of the Missouri Baptist Convention, he said to me, "Gene, a teacher of mine used to say: 'Never forget the three Fs. First, *find* the facts. Be certain that the evidence you have is factual, sufficiently factual as to be supported, if necessary, in a court of law.'

"'Then, *focus* the facts. Many an attorney has lost a case, not because he didn't have the facts in hand, but because he failed to have them in focus. He didn't know what he had.'

"'Finally, *follow* the facts. They will never lie.'" I have never forgotten this valuable advice, and it has served me as well in life as it has in research.

I wanted this work to be something that was practical, something that would stimulate an implementation of the daily, practical workings of the Spirit into the mind and life of the reading believer. In other words, I want it to help believers not only to understand the nature of the Holy Spirit, but, at the same time to allow Him to exercise His aliveness in and through them while knowing that such is possible without external excesses. *Alive in the Spirit!* works to produce a *MAN ALIVE!* Hopefully, I shall serve the reader in depicting some of the practical works the Holy Spirit performs in the believer's life.

Some information is simply not available. The Bible is often silent. One woman asked, "What will be the work of the Spirit in eternity?" I simply do not know. I can only assume (and assumptions can be dangerous) that He will be and do at least what He was and *did* in eternity past.

In many ways the book could well have been expanded. Expansion, however, is often the germ of defeat, as we bog down endlessly in minutiae. I want this book to be read and

⬛ PREFACE ⬛

understood and implemented into believers' lives, not just become "another book on the shelf."

As no book is entirely one's own, many are those to whom I owe much in the production of this work: to the Rev. Dr. James O. Parks, historian, for his provision of the material found in *Appendix B;* to Sarah Funderburke and her editors at Liberty Press who meticulously scrutinized the manuscript and offered many helpful suggestions; and to my dear wife, Rose Marie, for her prayers, wise counsel, and endless support. My prayer is that the Lord will abundantly bless this team effort, building up all of His servants unto "the praise of His glory" until He comes again!

Gene L. Jeffries
Springdale, Arkansas

ALIVE IN THE SPIRIT

CONTENTS

1	WHO IS THE HOLY SPIRIT?	1
2	THE SPIRIT CONVICTS	5
3	WHAT CONVERSION MEANS	11
4	HOW THE SPIRIT CONVERTS	17
5	LOVE COMES WITH CONVERSION	23
6	THE HOLY SPIRIT INDWELLS BELIEVERS	29
7	THE HOLY SPIRIT AND PRAYER	37
8	CONFESSION OF SIN	45
9	GIFTS OF THE SPIRIT: The *Serving* Gifts	53
10	GIFTS OF THE SPIRIT: The *Speaking* Gifts	61
11	GIFTS OF THE SPIRIT: The *Sign* Gifts	65
12	WHAT ABOUT "TONGUES?"	71
13	GLORIFYING CHRIST!	75
Appendix A	"TONGUES"	79
Appendix B	"HISTORICAL SYNOPSIS OF TONGUES-SPEAKING"	93
Bibliography		101

1

WHO IS THE HOLY SPIRIT?

William Shakespeare said, "All the world is a stage, the men and women are merely players."[1] In one sense he was right. But closer to the truth was the one who said,

> The center stage of world history, when seen from a Christian perspective, is not dominated by class struggles, race wars, or the whim of potentates, but is flooded with light and meaning from the lives of simple believers in the Most High God.[2]

The world is a stage. But, men and women are more than players; yet they are not the principal players. The three principal players are the members of the Trinity: God the Father, God the Son, and God the Holy Spirit. In the Old Testament era, God the Father was the Principal Personality. He stood, as it were, center stage. The Son and the Spirit were present, but they stood, as it were, in the wings of the stage.

---

1 William Shakespeare, *As You Like It*, Act 2, Scene 2.

2 Marshall Foster and Mary-Elaine Swanson, *The American Covenant* (Thousand Oaks, CA: Foundation for Christian Self-Government, 1981).

ALIVE IN THE SPIRIT

They made appearances now and then, but it was God the Father who was principal.

In the New Testament era, God the Son was the principal personality. He then stood center stage, while the Father and the Spirit stood in the wings. The most momentous event in human history was the cross of Jesus Christ! It was there that He worked divine redemption for all mankind, shedding His blood for the remission of man's sin and tasting death for every man.

The most incontrovertible fact of human history is the resurrection of Jesus Christ from the dead! In this singularly spectacular event, Jesus Christ proved that His life was infinitely superior to anything known to man. And in the practical combination of these events, Jesus Christ demonstrated His love by extending to sinful man the opportunity to exchange his life for the Divine Life that overcame death. The Father and the Spirit are as present in New Testament times as Christ was in the Old Testament times. But, They position Themselves offstage, making only incidental appearances.

Subsequent to Jesus Christ's resurrection appearances, He ascended into Heaven to assume His position as our Advocate at the right hand of the Father. Upon Christ's withdrawal from the earthly scene, the Holy Spirit descended to usher in the Church Age. Now, since that first-century Pentecost, man has been living in the era of the Holy Spirit. The Spirit is now center stage, and the Father and Son wait patiently in the wings until the coming of the end of this age.

Exactly who is the Holy Spirit and what does He do? Perhaps no personality has been more misunderstood than the Holy Spirit. Simultaneously, perhaps no work has been so misunderstood as His. Simply put, God the Holy Spirit is

▪ WHO IS THE HOLY SPIRIT? ▪

the third Person of the Triune Godhead. But how can God be "three" and "one" at the same time? While no analogy is adequate to describe the nature of the Trinity,[3] there is one that comes close. I am a son, a husband, and a father; yet, I am but one. To my father, I am his son. To my wife, I am her husband. To my son, I am his father. Still, I am the same, singular person. What is different is my "role," my "personality," alternately in each situation. I do not demonstrate the subservience to my son that I show to my father. I do not demonstrate the same kind of love to my father that I do to my wife. And I certainly do not exercise the authority over my father that I do over my son.

The problem with this analogy is that I have to "quick-change" my roles. God does not. He is simultaneously always Father, always Son, and always Holy Spirit. He makes no "changes," for He is always in character. The Lord Jesus describes the Holy Spirit as *paraklatos*, "Comforter." Actually, "Comforter" is more what He does than who He is. The Greek word means, "one called alongside." Certainly, alongside us, He exercises the strength and comfort and encouragement we need to face the rigorous experiences of life. Make no mistake about it: the Holy Spirit is God. He is as much God as God the Father and God the Son — but no more God than They.

Perhaps a note of caution should be sounded at this juncture. There are some who attempt to "polarize" the Trinity, giving greater honor to one of the Three-in-One. Some recognize only the Father. To them the Son and the Spirit are outside the deity. Others would say the same for the Son, relegating the Father and the Spirit to a level of "influence" that is less than personality. Then, there are those who believe in the Trinity,

---

[3] The Trinity is the belief that the Godhead is three personalities in one God as distinct from three gods.

but center all their theology in the Holy Spirit Himself. They would not deny a place to the Father or the Son, but give what would appear to be undue emphasis to the Spirit. The key to the doctrine of the Trinity is to allow the balance God Himself intended.

Still, what does the Holy Spirit do?

2

THE HOLY SPIRIT CONVICTS

We can rejoice that the Holy Spirit does convict! Otherwise, none of us would have hope. Nor do we in the least deserve the hope He offers. His love and graciousness are equal to the love and graciousness of the Father, who gave His Son, and equal to that of the Son, who gave His life.

The initial work of the Holy Spirit as He engages sinners is to convict them of their sin. As a teenager, I so clearly remember a tavern owner who came to hear me preach. As I pled with people to give their hearts to Christ, he gripped the back of the pew in front of him and wept openly. "Look," some said, "Joe's under conviction." But, was he? Seeing his knuckles white under a heavy grip and his face awash with tears may have indicated that conviction was present; but, those things in themselves do not constitute conviction. The Lord Jesus said,

> *And He, when He comes, will convict the world concerning sin, and righteousness, and judgment* (John 16:8).

The word translated "convict" (ελεγξει) means "to rebuke another with such evident truth as to bring him to the clear-sightedness of his sin."

With equal clarity I remember that Sunday morning in a small south Missouri church. Five children, ranging in age from nine to eleven, confessed their sins and received Jesus Christ as their Lord and Savior. The emotion of each differed markedly from the others. One little boy cried quite heavily. A girl cried, but quietly. Another boy smiled sweetly as I spoke with him. One was absolutely emotionless!

"Why did you come forward this morning?" I asked him.

"To ask Jesus into my heart," he said with a pokered expression. Nothing I asked or said moved him from that stoic state.

One-by-one I spoke with them. Each possessed his own personality and responded according to his own emotional construction. Yet, each one professed to have truly believed upon the Lord Jesus Christ and to have received Him as Savior. Emotions may be present; but they are not the conviction. They may indicate that something is going on inside; but, they themselves have no bearing upon the spiritual transformation of one's life. That is the work of the Holy Spirit alone.

When the Lord Jesus said that the Holy Spirit would "convict the world concerning sin," He meant that the Holy Spirit would use the Truth of God — His inerrant, infallible Word — to rebuke his humans creation so as to cause them to see their basic sin: the sin of not believing upon Jesus Christ as their Lord and Savior.

It is the Spirit who convinces men and women that their sin is more than not living up to standards of a good life and/or failing to rise above some of the social evils of the day. It

■ THE HOLY SPIRIT CONVICTS ■

is He who demonstrates to them that sin is one's personal displacement from the position for which God created him.

God sees every person either "in Adam" or "in Christ." Since Adam's sin in the Garden of Eden, all mankind has been born into sin and, therefore, needs deliverance. Christ came to be humanity's Deliverer from sin. The Father offered His only begotten Son, Jesus Christ, to die on the Cross for sin. Loving humanity more than His own life, Christ Jesus offered Himself. The Holy Spirit now works to convince every individual that Jesus Christ is the Father's only way for His creation to be saved from the family of Adam — a family of sin.

Reduced to the lowest theological denominator, an individual's severest sin is that of not receiving the Lord Jesus Christ as personal Savior.

> *He who believes in Him is not judged; he who does not believe has been judged already, because he has not believed in the name of the only begotten Son of God* (John 3:18).

The only channel by which any person of any age can ever be saved from sin is through the person of the Lord Jesus Christ (Acts 4:12). And it is the prime business of the Holy Spirit, when working with sinners, to convince them that they must receive Christ or spend eternity in Hell and separated from God.

At the same time, the Holy Spirit persuades the unbeliever of the righteousness of Jesus Christ. When the Rich Young Ruler arrested Jesus with his cry, "Teacher, what good thing shall I do that I may obtain eternal life?" Jesus responded,

> *"Why are you asking Me about what is good? There is only One who is good..."* (Matthew 19:17).

In effect, the Lord Jesus was asking, "Do you truly recognize Me as God, or are you simply being polite in your inquiry?"

Many today, who would not think of being impertinent toward God, fall short of believing that Jesus is "both Lord and Christ" (Acts 2:36). In point of fact, the Apostle Paul says that "no one can say, 'Jesus is Lord,' except by the Holy Spirit" (I Corinthians 12:3b). And the Apostle Peter assures us that Christ "committed no sin, nor was any deceit found in His mouth" (I Peter 2:22).

Peter's assurance is underwritten by the Holy Spirit who inspired the writings of Holy Scripture. Simultaneously, the inspired Word witnesses in connection with the witness of the Holy Spirit to bring the unbeliever to a point of trust — trust that Jesus is indeed God's Righteous One, God Himself.

In a trilogy of balance, the Holy Spirit labors also to convince unbelievers that they will face God Almighty on a day of judgment. You cannot do wrong and get by. "Be sure your sin will find you out" (Numbers 32:23), while a pronouncement to Israel, is an eternal principle to every people.

> *Do not be deceived, God is not mocked; for whatever a man sows, this he will also reap* (Galatians 6:7).

Somehow, deep within each of us (because we are so created) is the awareness that wrongs we do certainly require an accounting.[1] Rather than deny this wrong (although some try), people more frequently seek to balance the scales with human works of righteousness. Despite the Word of God to the contrary, people seek to proliferate their good works to

---

[1] In Romans 1:19–20, Paul implies that the nature of God is such that no one can fully know Him; yet, He provides sufficient Self-disclosure so that everyone is without excuse in acknowledging Him as Lord.

⋅ THE HOLY SPIRIT CONVICTS ⋅

such an extent that God will feel obliged to overlook their evil works. Yet, the Scriptures say,

> *He saved us, not on the basis of deeds which we have done in righteousness, but according to His mercy* (Titus 3:5).

It is the Holy Spirit, working somewhat in conjunction with an individual's conscience, who alone is qualified to convince everyone that they must someday stand before God in judgment.

What work can the Holy Spirit accomplish that will provide an escape from God's judgment? He converts individuals from their position in sin to a new position in Christ. But, what is conversion?

ALIVE IN THE SPIRIT

3

WHAT CONVERSION MEANS

No more sobering thought has ever been put into verse than by Robert Harkness.

Why should He love me so?
Why should He love me so?
Why should my Savior to Calvary go?
Why should He love me so?

Although far from simple, there is some understanding of "why" given from Scripture. It is important to understand that the "holy war" exists between the Lord and Satan, not between Satan and the Lord's redeemed.

Before God created man, He created the angels. They existed to praise Him and to perform His will.[1] When Lucifer, the Archangel, rebelled against God, he persuaded myriads of

---

[1] See Isaiah 14:12ff and Ezekiel 28:12ff for a discussion of the nature and activity of unfallen angels.

angels to follow him in his rebellion.² The resultant activity of God was to forbid them further residence in Heaven and further access to Him. Now, Satan laughed, charging God with not being able to maintain order within His creation.

Subsequently, God created humanity that they might worship and serve Him. But again, Satan sought to thwart God's plan by lying to Eve:

> *"You surely shall not die! For God knows that in the day you eat from it [the tree of the knowledge of good and evil] your eyes will be opened, and you will be like God, knowing good and evil"* (Genesis 3:4-5).

Now, Satan laughed most haughtily! God could keep neither the angels nor man — both of whom He created— under control, he charged.

Had the Lord's plan been merely to *save* humanity and take all to Heaven, He would doubtlessly have done so immediately. His plan, however, included much more. Not only would He provide a means to save humanity from Hell and take many to Heaven, the Lord would leave humanity on Earth to demonstrate in the most vivid manner possible that He Himself was Lord indeed, and that humanity was here to be "to the praise of His glory" (Ephesians 1:12).

Conversion means "the act of turning with" someone. In this instance, unbelievers, now convinced of their own sin, convinced of Jesus Christ's absolute righteousness, and convinced of the Father's coming judgment, turn toward Christ by the Holy Spirit's power.

---

2 Although we have no knowledge of the precise number of angels God created, the rebellion resulted in one-third of them being expelled from Heaven and from access to God. See Revelation 12:4.

▰ WHAT CONVERSION MEANS ▰

Could there be any greater conceivable tragedy than to know yourself to be a sinner and to know that Jesus Christ is capable of saving you from sin, and yet not to possess the key to the experience of salvation? God has not left us without hope! The same Holy Spirit, who convicts us of sin, righteousness and judgment, converts us from the family of Adam into the family of Christ.

When Paul and Silas were in prison in Philippi, God sent an earthquake "so that the foundations of the prison house were shaken" (Acts 16:26). It pleases me to believe that this is not only literally true, but emblematic of how God the Holy Spirit works within us by getting to the root of the sin problem.

Our nature needs converting. We are living in a day of spectacular medical achievements. Heart transplants were hardly a dream only a few years ago. Now, medical science is advancing at such a pace that where human hearts are unavailable for transplantation, surgeons utilize an artificial heart! Still, our most fundamental need is not for a heart transplant, but for a heart *transformation!* And such is the work of the Holy Spirit.

Several years ago, I had the privilege of speaking to a large gathering of Rotarians in Auckland, New Zealand. Oddly enough, and without my knowledge, I had been booked to speak on the subject "Race Relations in the South U.S.A." I objected, saying that I had never lived in the deep south and was totally unfamiliar with racial difficulties. My plea fell on deaf ears. "You have been booked under that subject," my host said, "and the only alternative is to cancel your appearance." Not wanting to miss such a golden opportunity, I reluctantly agreed. I virtually prepared my remarks en route to the meeting. Viewed by my audience as an "expert" (as are all Americans when away from home!), I proceeded to share a few historical thoughts that approached my subject. Then, with a burst of enlightenment that could only have come from the Holy Spirit Himself, I said, "Gentlemen, I have the answer to the race problem in America and throughout the world!" My audience snapped to brisk attention. "Man needs a change in his nature," I said. "He needs a racially unbiased heart. And when man sees his bias as sin, and repents and believes upon Jesus Christ, Christ changes man's heart. Man needs to be born again."

Rotary speakers worldwide are subjected to a friendly interrogation by their audiences. Had I written out questions for them to ask me, my questions could not have been better than their own. "Why do you insist that Jesus Christ is the solution?" one man asked. "What do you mean by 'born again?'" inquired another. It was an incredible evening!

Humanity's need has not changed. Our nature needs converting because it is corrupt in its thought. Genesis 6:5 describes the days of Noah as so inherently evil that "...every intent of the thoughts of his [man's] heart was only evil continually."

Our world today is not far from that mark. We lived for a while in the New York City area. The nightly local news was more gruesome than the nightly network news. When you realize that the news that makes the networks is local news first and that the pool of information is a plethora of perils, you can grasp some idea of why network news is so often gruesome. Such is the nature of humanity without Christ.

Human nature is corrupt in its affection. Paul wrote his protégé, Timothy, "...for Demas, having loved this present world, has deserted me..." (II Timothy 4:10a).

Before individuals encounter Jesus Christ in the new birth experience, their affections are centered on the material

WHAT CONVERSION MEANS

pleasures and aspects of this present world. To be sure, these desires vary; but, it is fair to say that the goals and dreams of the unbeliever are focused on things of this world.

Riding in a posh car down an Australian street, I expressed to the owner how pleasurable it was to ride in such luxury. "Yes," he said, "all I ever told the Lord I wanted was a nice house and a nice car." His remarks betrayed the focus of his affection.

Further still, human nature is corrupt in its will. The Lord Jesus said, "And you are unwilling to come to Me, that you may have life" (John 5:40).

Humanity's failure to emigrate to Christ is a matter of the will. It is not that individuals cannot be saved; they do not want to be. It may be that a person lacks the knowledge of the need to be saved or that another knows the need and simply does not want it. But in either event, it is not that Christ Jesus is unable or indisposed, but that the individual himself is unwilling to be saved. Each one must will to come to Christ. Failure to will to be in Christ leads logically and naturally to one's failure to be in Christ. It all starts with the will. We must will to receive Christ, but the Holy Spirit actually does the converting, as we shall see in the next chapter.

ALIVE IN THE SPIRIT

4

HOW THE SPIRIT CONVERTS

As the work of the Holy Spirit with sinners is to convict them of their sin of not being "in Christ," so His work extends to actually converting them to Christ. John records the Lord Jesus' answer to Nicodemus' inquiry about being born again.

> *How can a man be born when he is old? He cannot enter a second time into his mother's womb and be born, can he?* (John 3:4)

Jesus' reply was forthright.

> *Truly, truly, I say to you, unless one is born of water and the Spirit, he cannot enter into the kingdom of God. That which is born of the flesh is flesh; and that which is born of the Spirit is spirit. Do not marvel that I said to you, "You must be born again"* (John 3:5-7).

The LORD's words have been variously interpreted; still, the Bible has always proved to be its own best commentary. When Christ spoke of the water-birth, He spoke of the physical birth which Nicodemus understood. When He spoke of the spiritual birth, He spoke of the new birth, the "birth from above." This

◾ ALIVE IN THE SPIRIT ◾

"birth from above" Nicodemus did not readily understand. One who is born physically needs to be born again spiritually. Of course, one who has never been born physically cannot be born "again" spiritually.

With His initiation of spiritual conversion in our lives, the Holy Spirit turns the balance of our human judgment.[1] We begin to see sin and righteousness as God sees them instead of how we have viewed them until now. When we are allowed to possess God's divine view on sin, we begin to understand how costly was the price of our salvation for the Heavenly Father. We also begin to understand the inestimable cost of the cross to our Savior!

Those so-called "menial" sins are no longer menial. It was they, as well as the gross sins like murder and adultery, that sent Christ to the Cross. Possessing something of the balanced human judgment God intended for man at Creation, we now see that all sin is big sin and all sin is forthrightly against God (Psalm 51:4). We understand what Judas Iscariot understood when he "saw that he had been condemned" (Matthew 27:3). We understand the reverberating remorse of King David when he cried, "I have sinned!" (II Samuel 12:13).

Simultaneously with conversion, the Holy Spirit commences to turn the bias of our will. The imbalance of human judgment prior to conversion automatically biases the will against God and that which is godly. The Holy Spirit changes that. He biases our converted wills toward Christ. Nothing matters now except Christ and His holiness.

Nothing more, nothing less, nothing else — at any cost! The Psalmist puts it clearly into perspective,

---

[1] For a full discussion on this subject, see Joseph Alleine's *An Alarm to the Unconverted* (London: The Banner of Truth Trust, 1959), 26f.

▪ HOW THE SPIRIT CONVERTS ▪

Let Thy hand be ready to help me,
For I have chosen Thy precepts (Psalm 119:173 ASV)

Here is the believer-soldier who has enlisted for the duration of the war. *Wherever I go, whatever I am destined to encounter, just help me, Lord; for I have elected to do whatever You assign me.*

Far from the reckless abandon of the unsaved to the ways of sin, the believer in Christ Jesus is led by the indwelling Holy Spirit to accomplish the Father's work on Earth until Jesus comes again. What the world thinks does not matter. What other believers think does not matter. The believer is encouraged by the Holy Spirit to engage in the activities He Himself elects.

Several years ago, the Lord led us into full-time evangelistic work in Australia. We had very little money and knew only to appeal to other believers for help. I mailed scores of letters of appeal to pastors and churches, concluding with the words of Paul,

Not that I seek the gift itself, but I seek for the profit which increases to your account (Philippians 4:17).

Subsequent perusal and meditation helped me understand that while I was certainly endeavoring to be true to the Lord's calling on my life and ministry, my motive in solicitation of funds were less pure than Paul's. What stunned me more at the time, however, were the responses! All but two were negative! Some of my pastor-friends even suggested that if, indeed, the Australians wanted my ministry in their country they ought to be willing to provide me with a house for my family, a car for my travel, and a salary for our living.

What was missing in my motive in soliciting travel funds was balanced by my enthusiasm to do what the LORD had surely called us to do! It was not the reckless abandon some supposed. It was obedience to the LORD's leadership. It was a bias toward His will.

At the conclusion of our first year in Australia, the LORD had provided funds equal to what we had surrendered when we resigned the "security" of the pastorate. The ministry the LORD gave us in Australia far exceeded anything I could have possibly imagined! At the end of our tenure, the records revealed that more than 5000 persons had committed themselves to Jesus Christ for salvation and that many more had either renewed their dedication to the LORD or surrendered to some form of full-time Christian ministry! And those two, positive churches that responded faithfully, one with $25.00 per month for five years, shared in the fruit that abounded to its account!

The Holy Spirit simultaneously turns the bent of the believer's affection. The question of which was the greatest commandment was posited to the Lord Jesus. He replied in a quotation from Deuteronomy 6:5 that summarized the Ten Commandments:

> "You shall love the Lord your God with all your heart, and with all your soul, and with all your mind." This is the great and foremost commandment. The second is like it, "You shall love your neighbor as yourself" (Matthew 22:37-39).

As the Spirit turns the bent of the affections, the believer's desire is changed. Those "things" we once loved, we now find ourselves despising. What we thought we could not get along without, now hardly matters at all. Habits we knew we could not live without suddenly vanished; and we had to try to remember that they were a part of our lives at all. The Apostle Paul also experienced this turn in the bent of his affections.

■ HOW THE SPIRIT CONVERTS ■

> *But whatever things were gain to me, those things I have counted as loss for the sake of Christ. More than that, I count all things to be loss in view of the surpassing value of knowing Christ Jesus my Lord, for whom I have suffered the loss of all things, and count them but rubbish in order that I may gain Christ, and may be found in Him, not having a righteousness of my own, derived from the Law, but that which is through faith in Christ, the righteousness which comes from God on the basis of faith...* (Philippians 3:7-9).

Dr. Jeanette Beal, one of the early American missionary-physicians to enter China, once related to me that a Chinese man she knew was delivered from opium addiction following his acceptance of Christ. She had never seen before or since anyone delivered from opium addiction; but that man was. And it was by the power of God that he was delivered. His desire was changed forever!

Joys, too, are changed. Before his conversion to Christ, Saul of Tarsus' "joy" emerged from his harassment of believers in Christ. Following his conversion, however, he wrote that his joy rested in Christ — a joy he willingly shared with fellow believers.

> *But even if I am being poured out as a drink offering upon the sacrifice and service of your faith, I rejoice and share my joy with you all* (Philippians 2:17).

Someone once pointed out to me that the difference between joy and happiness was that happiness depends upon "happenings," whereas joy is the consciousness of the love of God toward us in Christ Jesus. Paul was more than happy; he was joyous! For the focus of his life now centered upon Christ, who is the source of all genuine joy.

≽ ALIVE IN THE SPIRIT ≼

In the next chapter, we shall learn what major attribute of Christ comes with conversion.

5

LOVE COMES WITH CONVERSION

Acceptance of the Lord Jesus Christ as your Savior allows the Holy Spirit to alter the cares of your life. Life abounds with cares! A preacher-friend of mine once said, "Either you're in trouble, or you're coming out of trouble, or you're headed for trouble!" Sounds like the story of human life. Paul wrote that trouble is everywhere.

We are afflicted in every way, but not crushed; perplexed, but not despairing; persecuted, but not forsaken; struck down, but not destroyed; ... For we who live are constantly being delivered over to death for Jesus' sake... (II Corinthians 4:8-11).

Paul's expectation of trouble, however, was not dampening to his spirit; for Paul looked beyond his immediate circumstances to the hope that the Holy Spirit held before him. His cares were altered.

For I consider that the sufferings of this present time are not worthy to be compared with the glory that is to be revealed to us (Romans 8:18).

■ ALIVE IN THE SPIRIT ■

The strongest of humanistic philosophies pales before the Christian philosophy of the great Apostle. Paul was no existentialist![1] The redemption Christ had accomplished for Paul gave meaning to the past, the present, and the future. Were we to allow the Holy Spirit the same liberty with our lives, the brilliance of a future with Christ would ease the pains of the present — pains we too often grumblingly endure. Let us remember that the Holy Spirit who alters our cares is the same as He who changed our joys.

President Franklin D. Roosevelt once noted that "The only thing we have to fear is fear itself." Fear in the spiritual realm, however, is not always to be avoided. It is true that the Psalmist prayed and his fears were assuaged. His were human fears of a human dilemma.

> *I sought the Lord and He answered me,*
> *And delivered me from all my fears* (Psalm 34:4).

But, there is a reverential fear of God that is spiritually healthy. Solomon experimented with life in his futile effort to extract meaning from humanity itself. His conclusion denounces his humanistic endeavors in favor of God's eternal plan.

> *The conclusion, when all has been heard, is: fear God and keep His commandments, because this applies to every person* (Ecclesiastes 12:13).

In addition to all of the above, the Holy Spirit gives you a new love. Far more than a reconditioning of your old love, this

---

[1] Existentialism is a relatively recent radical departure in philosophy. It views man's innate power in the realms of reason and of the heart. Fundamentally, existentialism's thesis is that man's existence is prior to his essence. For a brief treatment of this subject, see "Existentialism" in Bernard Ramm's *A Handbook of Contemporary Theology* (Grand Rapids: William B. Eerdmans Publishing Company, 1966), 46-47.

≡ LOVE COMES WITH CONVERSION ≡

new love is His Love — *agape* — surging through your veins!

Human love is a lot like human happiness: it hinges on whether someone else loves us. We often live out the Golden Rule as if it read, "Do unto others *as they do* unto you." Or, "Do unto others *because they have done* unto you." Some even read it as saying, "Do unto others *before* they do unto you."

The powers of rationalization come upon us early in life. I can remember well being mistreated by another boy and saying to my mother, "Well, he knows the Golden Rule. If that's how he's going to treat me, it must be the way he wants me to treat him!" Read the Golden Rule without mirrors!

When the Holy Spirit replaces our human love with Christ's divine love, dramatic changes result! Appropriately, the Apostle John, the apostle of love, warns us against making the world and its enterprises the object of our love.

> *Do not love the world, nor the things in the world. If anyone loves the world, the love of the Father is not in him*
> (I John 2:15).

Perhaps John recalled the Psalmist's warning about loving God in times when human complaints might seem justified.

> *O love the Lord, all you His godly ones!*
> *The Lord preserves the faithful,*
> *And fully recompenses the proud doer.*
> *Be strong, and let your heart take courage,*
> *All you who hope in the LORD*
> *(Psalm 31:23-24).*

The antithesis of love is hate. Interestingly, God does not replace our capacity for hatred; rather, He refocuses it. We are to love those people we previously hated and hate those things we previously loved.

▪ ALIVE IN THE SPIRIT ▪

You have heard that it was said, "You shall love your neighbor, and hate your enemy." But I say to you, love your enemies, and pray for those who persecute you" (Matthew 5:43-44).

Jude incites us to hate "even the garment polluted by the flesh" (Jude 23).

We are to hate sin passionately because of the price it required of God. "The price of sin was so great that only God could pay it. The price of sin was so great that not even God could pay it again."[2]

Not the least of the "bendings" brought against our affection is that of human sorrow. The Holy Spirit refuses to erase sorrow; but He works quickly to redirect the object of it.

The Apostle Paul wrote at least four separate epistles to the Corinthian Church. Two of the four have been preserved for us in the Bible. And the two epistles we have, make reference to the two we do not have.[3] One of the lost epistles was connoted the "sorrowful" epistle. What Paul said to the Corinthians in that epistle caused them great sorrow. But, that sorrow worked out to their good, as Paul is careful to show.

For though I caused you sorrow by my letter, I do not regret it — for I see that that letter caused you sorrow, though only for a while — I now rejoice, not that you were made

---

2 The late George D. Thomason, Th.D., Chapel Service, Midwestern Baptist Theological Seminary, 1960.

3 Paul wrote at least four separate epistles to the Corinthian Church. The one we call First Corinthians, is his *second;* and the one we call Second Corinthians, is his *fourth.* For a more complete discussion of this, see "Lost Letter" in Robert Gromacki's *New Testament Survey* (Grand Rapids: Baker Book House, 1974), 203-204.

▰ LOVE COMES WITH CONVERSION ▰

> *sorrowful, but that you were made sorrowful to the point of repentance; for you were made sorrowful according to the will of God, in order that you might not suffer loss in anything through us. For the sorrow that is according to the will of God produces a repentance without regret, leading to salvation; but the sorrow of the world produces death* (II Corinthians 7:8-10).

Has the Spirit of God convicted your heart and life of sin? Has He shown you how your sin sent Jesus Christ to the Cross of Calvary? You can experience His spiritual power that changes human lives! Confess your sin to Him in prayer. Ask for His forgiveness. Believe that He will perform in your life what He promises in His Word,

> *Believe in the Lord Jesus and you shall be saved, you and your household* (Acts 16:31).

If you've never trusted Christ, pray this prayer to Him right now:

> Dear Lord, I know that I am a sinner. I know I've done many wrong things in my life. I'm sorry for my sin. I know that Jesus loves me, and that He died and rose again to save me from my sin. Right now, in my heart, I willingly turn from my sin. And by faith I receive the Lord Jesus Christ as my Savior. In Jesus' name I pray. Amen.

Once you have believed in Christ, the Holy Spirit comes to permanently indwell your life. In the next chapter we shall examine the many benefits of this indwelling.

ALIVE IN THE SPIRIT

6

THE HOLY SPIRIT INDWELLS BELIEVERS

A theological definition of the baptism of the Holy Spirit is vital at this point. When Paul wrote to the Corinthian Church about this baptism, he said,

For by one Spirit we were all baptized into one body, whether Jews or Greeks, whether slaves or free, and we were all made to drink of one Spirit (I Corinthians 12:13).

The baptism of the Holy Spirit is the spiritual act whereby the Holy Spirit immerses the one believing upon Jesus into the body of Christ. It is at this moment that he becomes a true believer, a genuine Christian. And it is at this point that the Holy Spirit assumes immediate residency in the believer's life. Spirit baptism regards the believer's relationship to Christ.

Do you not know that you are a temple of God, and that the Spirit of God dwells in you? If any man destroys the temple of God, God will destroy him, for the temple of God is holy, and that is what you are (I Corinthians 3:16-17).

■ ALIVE IN THE SPIRIT ■

The apostle reaffirms this truth in I Corinthians 6:19-20 and again in Ephesians 2:19-22. The Holy Spirit is not like a coat that can be put on and off according to the wearer's desire. Once the Spirit has taken up residency within the believer, He expects to remain — and to remain in control! Salvation is both immediate and ongoing. Snatched from the penalty of death due to sin, the believer must also be continually snatched from the power of sin that would exercise daily control over his life. This ongoing salvation is part of the Holy Spirit's work.

That the Holy Spirit never departs from the believer once He has assumed residency in the believer's life is biblically defensible.

When the Lord commissioned Moses to deliver Israel from her imprisonment in Egypt, Moses objected, asking, "Who am I?" The Lord's response was, "Certainly, I will be with you..." But, Moses protested asking, "What shall I say to Israel when she asks me, 'What is His name?' What shall I say to them?"

> *And God said to Moses, "I AM WHO I AM"; and He said, "Thus you shall say to the sons of Israel, 'I AM has sent me to you'"* (Exodus 3:14).

The Hebrew for "I AM WHO I AM" literally means "I AM God, and I AM all that you need Me to be in any given situation."[1]

At the same time the Spirit takes up permanent residency within the born-again believer, He desires to control the believer with the view toward making him into the likeness of Jesus Christ.

When the Lord gave the Ten Commandments to Israel

---

1 See יהוה (YHWH) *in locus, Kittel's Theological Dictionary.*

▪ THE HOLY SPIRIT INDWELLS BELIEVERS ▪

through Moses, He stated His rightful jealousy over His people. "You shall have no other gods before Me" (Exodus 20:3). And just as the Lord had the right to expect His people (Israel) to maintain allegiance toward Him, so the Holy Spirit has the right to expect the Church (all believers) to maintain allegiance toward Him.

The Apostle James, therefore, indicates the Spirit's attitude toward the Church, when he writes,

> *The Spirit who He has made to dwell in us jealously desires us* (James 4:5, paraphrase).

It is the Lord's intention that we, His church, should "be to the praise of His glory" just as Israel was to have been.[2]

The Holy Spirit is a person. We should refer to Him appropriately as "He" or "Him," never "it." Draper says,

> He has a mind, for He is intelligent. He has knowledge, wisdom, and reasoning. He has a will. In His will He acts, He decides, He chooses.... . He has all of the characteristics and actions of a person.[3]

As a person, He is not divisible. That is, there is no such thing as one possessing only a portion of the Holy Spirit. One would not say of a minister, "Part of him preached a sermon last Sunday morning." The minister is a whole person, and he must not be divided into parts during his sermon delivery (or afterwards, for that matter). His spirit, soul and body are all jointly involved. Even so, at the point of conversion, the believer receives all of the Holy Spirit in that very instant!

---

[2] Study Isaiah 43:21 and related passages.

[3] James T. Draper, Jr. *Foundations of Biblical Faith* (Nashville: Broadman Press, 1979), 36.

ALIVE IN THE SPIRIT

The word translated "filling" (πληρου/σθε) must be viewed with respect to the Spirit's control over the believer. Our English word is misleading in that it begs to know some measure — a third, a fourth, a half. As a person, the Holy Spirit cannot suffer division.

> ...for [God] gives the Spirit without measure... (John 3:34).

"Filling," therefore, is best understood as the Spirit's control in regards to the believer's fellowship with Christ.

Indwelling the believer, the Holy Spirit guarantees redemption.

> *In Him, you also, after listening to the message of truth, the gospel of your salvation — having also believed, you were sealed in Him with the Holy Spirit of promise, who is given as a pledge of our inheritance, with a view to the redemption of God's own possession, to the praise of His glory* (Ephesians 1:13-14).

Two important notations regarding the Holy Spirit lie in these two verses. First, the Holy Spirit is viewed as God's "Seal" upon the believer. The Greek word τω allows the dative, the locative or the instrumental case. If dative, it would say "sealed *to* the Spirit"; if locative, "sealed *in* the Spirit"; or if instrumental, "sealed *with* (or *by*) the Spirit." Yet, inasmuch as Paul is discussing here the Ephesians' reception of the Spirit at the time of their hearing of the Gospel, it seems best to understand Paul as saying that this is the Father's activity of securing us "in Christ" by putting the Holy Spirit upon us as the Father's seal. That the Spirit is *Himself the Seal* seems evident also from II Corinthians 1:21-22:

> *Now He who establishes us with you in Christ and anointed us is God, who also sealed us and gave us the Spirit in our hearts as a pledge.*

■ THE HOLY SPIRIT INDWELLS BELIEVERS ■

There is an analogy to this in the double-ring marriage ceremony: when we hear the Gospel and receive the Lord Jesus Christ, God immediately dispenses His Holy Spirit to establish residence within us (God's "ring" to [or seal upon] us). In turn, we respond by identifying with Him outwardly through water baptism (our "ring" or pledge to God).

Several years ago, I had the privilege of viewing the mission work of New Tribes Mission in Papua New Guinea. In that brief time, I became acquainted with several cultural characteristics unique to the tribal people. One of the more interesting regarded the way in which dating and marriage takes place. A fellow from one tribe sees a girl from another tribe whom he would like to have as a wife. And he says, "Me mark finish." When I first heard the expression, I thought he was telling her his name: Mark Finish. Rather it is an expression to the girl in Pidgin English, the trade language, that means, "I have seen you; I have marked you for my own; and that's the end of it!"

Now, truly there is more to the process of engagement and marriage that just those words; but how wonderfully they illustrate what transpires between God and the believer. God sees us in our sinful state and determines through Jesus Christ's death on the Cross to save us. When we believe upon Christ, the Father "marks" us as His own with His Holy Spirit. And that is the end of it so far as security in Him is concerned. Surely, this was included in the thinking of Christ Jesus when He cried from the Cross, "It is finished."

The believer is eternally and positionally secure in Christ. And the presence of the Holy Spirit is the "mark" of that security, just as the rainbow is the "mark" from God — His promise to never again destroy the world by a flood.

Those who advocate that someone can become "lost"

after having been "saved" through redemption in Christ Jesus miss the point and means of redemption. God is the Redeemer. What God redeems, He secures in that redemption. There is only one possible means of two supposed ways of salvation: grace or works. If salvation be by grace, then it is of God and the security connected with that redemption is in God's Hands.

If, on the other hand, salvation be by works, then it is entirely up to the individual to maintain his salvation by continuously performing good works. Under the "works" plan, if anyone does good works, he is saved; if they cease or slip, they are lost — presumably forever, or until enough good works are completed to make up the deficit.

If man could be saved by good works, then the sacrificial death of Christ on the cross was totally without merit. Furthermore, God, who sent His Son to that cross (II Corinthians 5:21), then Himself committed the gravest mistake: for He gave Christ to die for humanity, who did not need His death — if indeed anyone could affect his own redemption. But, this is not possible.

From the practical standpoint, believing in one's own good works for salvation would be a horrendous way to live. Think of it! Never knowing whether you had stockpiled a sufficiency of good works to see you into the glorious side of eternity! And what if one had not! Now, on the deathbed one contemplates his own sin! "My sin is too great!" he declares. And with life too far spent and energies too far gone, it is impossible to conjure up more good works! What a pitiful theological view!

All the more we see how God affected for us what we could not procure for ourselves.

▬ THE HOLY SPIRIT INDWELLS BELIEVERS ▬

Amazing Grace, how sweet the sound,
That saved a wretch like me;
I once was lost, but now am found;
'Twas blind, but now I see.[4]

The indwelling Holy Spirit also guards the believer against the intrusion of sin. Once again the Apostle Paul instructs us from Galatians 5:17:

> *For the flesh sets its desire against the Spirit, and the Spirit against the flesh; for these are in opposition to one another, so that you may not do the things that you please.*

When I was in elementary school, we used to play a game at recess called "King of the Mountain." A smooth, rectangular stone that I am certain was intended to serve a better purpose, lay close to the sidewalk at the edge of the school ground. Whomever of the boys was first to ascend the twenty-inch-high stone assumed the position of authority. Once in place, he would strike a balanced pose that was intended to thwart others from forcing him off the stone. Usually, it was a short-lived position because the boys at the base of the stone would unite to topple the "king."

Yet, years later I thought back upon it as a superb illustration of the guardianship aspect of the Holy Spirit's work in the life of the believer. The Spirit assumes His position in our lives as *King* the moment we trust Jesus Christ as our Lord and Savior. Striking a balanced "pose" in our lives, He then fights to keep sin from invading us and exercising control over those faculties we surrendered to Christ.

With the Lord's deliverance of Israel from Egypt, He noted

---

[4] John Newton, a slave trader before his conversion to Christ, wrote these words that were later added to a traditional American melody.

for them in His commandments at Sinai that He was a jealous God — jealous over their love and affection.

> *You shall have no other gods before Me. You shall not make for yourself an idol.... You shall not worship them or serve them; for I, the LORD your God, am a jealous God...* (Exodus 20:3-5).

The Lord had the right to divine jealousy. Not only is His jealousy *inherently* right because He is God and can do no wrong, but because as Deliverer of Israel from Egypt, the Lord has "earned" the right through His redemption of His people.

James indicates that the Holy Spirit exercises a holy jealousy over New Testament believers in the same way the Father exercised His holy jealousy over Old Testament believers.

> *The Spirit whom He has made to dwell in us jealously desires us* (James 4:5, paraphrase).

It is well for us that the Holy Spirit both possesses and exercises that right. Look how bad we are with Him! Can you imagine what we would be without Him? Without the Holy Spirit, we would know no spiritual growth. As prayer is integral to the growth, we shall next explore the role of the Holy Spirit in the prayer in the life of the believer.

7

THE HOLY SPIRIT AND PRAYER

Further still, the Holy Spirit graduates our grace. When our Lord Jesus promised that the Holy Spirit would come, he clearly noted that the Spirit would lead believers into the full truths of God.

But when He, the Spirit of truth, comes, He will guide you into all truth... (John 16:13).

Paul verified Christ's promise by insisting that believers grow spiritually.

...be filled with the Spirit... (Ephesians 5:18).

Implicit in this insistence is that God the Holy Spirit is in charge of the believer's growth, and that the believer can indeed understand more and more about God and His overall divine plan.

Peter, however, is perhaps the most succinct when he admonishes the believer unto spiritual growth.

■ ALIVE IN THE SPIRIT ■

...but grow in the grace and knowledge of our Lord and Savior Jesus Christ (II Peter 3:18).

In any and every event, the Lord and His chief apostles expected and required born-again Christians to increase spiritually. In the same way it is unnatural for a physical child not to experience physical growth; it is unnatural for a spiritual child not to experience spiritual growth.

But, in what ways does the Holy Spirit assist us in growing spiritually? Hardly anything is more vital to the spiritual growth of a believer in Jesus Christ than prayer.

Before Robert Murray McCheyne died at the age of 30, he said, "If the veil of the world's machinery were lifted off, how much we would find is done in answer to the prayers of God's children."[1]

Unfortunately, we have the idea that when all else fails, we should resort to prayer. The truth is that most of what fails does so because we have not prayed. I have literally heard preachers say, "Well, we've done everything we can; now we must pray."

Certainly there is a "working side" not to be overlooked. The Scriptures and the example of biblical Christians teach us the indispensability of spiritual balance. Paul prayed "without ceasing" (I Thessalonians 5:17); at the same time, he physically journeyed into unevangelized areas and preached the Gospel. At times, he resorted to making and mending tents (a craft he had learned from his Jewish childhood) in order to sustain himself physically. Thus, balance was ever in view in his life.

---

1 Robert Murray McCheyne, as quoted by E. M. Bounds in *Power Through Prayer* (Grand Rapids: Zondervan Publishing House, 1965), 63.

✷ THE HOLY SPIRIT AND PRAYER ✷

Our error in this age is that we are works-oriented — in regards to salvation — but leave much to be desired in the works area once we have been saved. How can we honestly believe that Christ Jesus saved us by grace and allow prayer no more part in our lives than we do? No wonder there is such stunted growth in Christendom!

"But, I don't know how to pray!" someone says. Paul anticipated such an outcry when he wrote that the Holy Spirit is very much involved in spiritual prayer.

> *And in the same way the Spirit also helps our weakness; for we do not know how to pray as we should, but the Spirit Himself intercedes for us...* (Romans 8:26).

Can you imagine the power genuine, spiritual prayer could engender, were we to allow the Holy Spirit to help us in this area of critical weakness?

What really constitutes power-filled prayer? What is the secret of believers like praying Hyde and George Mueller and John Welch? Does the Holy Spirit work with believers today as He did with them? Indeed He does! And with the rest of us, He would like to! The foremost key involving the secret to answered prayer is found in John 15:7. Jesus said,

> *If you abide in Me, and My words abide in you, ask whatever you wish, and it shall be done for you.*

The analysis of this key verse is at the same time simple and quite difficult. It is simple to understand; it is quite difficult to live out. Part of the verse relates what we are to do and part relates what Christ will do.

The key word here is "abide." It means "to continue to stay, to dwell, to live, to lodge" in a particular realm. Jesus identifies Himself as that "realm" when He says, "...abide in Me." In other words, "to abide in Me" is to "relax and continually be at home in and with Christ." Solomon noted,

> *The name of the Lord is a strong tower;*
> *The righteous runs into it and is safe* (Proverbs 18:10).

Simultaneously, the believer must continually live in and by the Word of God, the Holy Scriptures. "...My words abide in you," means that in the same way that we continually find rest in Him, His words must find rest in us. We must learn His teachings and live out what we learn. The Psalmist wrote,

> *Thy word I have treasured in my heart,*
> *That I might not sin against Thee* (Psalm 119:11).

The word "if" in John 15:7 must be read, "If — maybe you will, maybe you won't." In any event, it is *conditional*. His promises are conditioned upon whether we live in Him and allow His words to permeate our innermost being.

When we "continually abide" in Him and allow His word to "continually abide" in us, we are where the Holy Spirit is able to use us in the Lord's service. The concept of "ask" presupposes the Holy Spirit's allowance. It is, in fact, the Spirit Himself who prompts us to "ask"; and it is He who determines "whatever we wish." Remember how Paul told us that the Spirit helped us in our weakness? Remember how he reminded us that we do not know what to ask and are dependent upon the Spirit to assist us?

We are prompted by the Holy Spirit to pray. The scriptural teaching is that all genuine prayer begins and ends with God. It begins with God the Holy Spirit and it ends with God the Father. To put it yet another way, God the Holy Spirit prays to God the Father— and He uses the Spirit-controlled believer as His avenue for prayer. In the way that a witch is a human medium for the transmission of a demon's messages on the

⚍ THE HOLY SPIRIT AND PRAYER ⚌

evil side, the Spirit-controlled, born-again believer is a human medium for the prayers of the Holy Spirit to God the Father on the righteous side.

Thus, the full import of the verse is that when we are in that spiritual position where we can be of benefit to the Holy Spirit, what He asks of the Father through us cannot be denied. Nor indeed, does the Father wish to deny what the Spirit asks. For They consistently demonstrate unity. The Spirit *cannot ask* what the Father *does not wish* to convey; and the Father *cannot deny* what is asked Him by the Spirit. Herein lies the key to answered prayer.

A student preacher was lecturing a seminary evangelism class on faith. He illustrated his subject with this story:

> A minister of a congregation had just concluded a stirring sermon on "faith." One of the congregation approached him saying, "That was a fine and enlightening sermon, Pastor; but tell me, what is faith?"
>
> Perplexed that the man had listened without learning, the minister quoted again from Hebrews 11:1, "Now faith is the substance of things hoped for, the evidence of things not seen."
>
> "Yes sir, I know — but what does that mean?"
>
> "Do you know Sister Jones?" the minister asked.
>
> "I sure do," the parishioner replied. "Everybody knows Sister Jones. She's got the best fried chicken in the whole county."
>
> "Well," said the minister, "last Sunday she invited me home to her house for dinner. And while we were sitting and waiting, Sister Jones' oldest girl came into the dining room

carrying a bowl of delicious chicken gravy!"

Both men smacked their lips at the thought, and the preacher concluded, "Now, brother, that is *FAITH!* For that is the substance of the thing that was hoped for!"

It is appropriate that the Epistle to the Hebrews should so heavily address the subject of faith. Throughout the eleventh chapter, one after another is summoned to testify of faith: the elders, Abel, Enoch, Noah, Abraham, Sarah, Isaac, Jacob, Joseph, Moses, Rahab, Gideon, Barak, Samson, Jephthah, David, Samuel and an innumerable host.

Yet, when we come to verse 39, careful investigation demonstrates that "the report" mentioned (v. 2) does not so much indicate a report on those listed as faithful throughout the chapter (although that, too, is true), as it indicates a revelation that God gave to each one prior to his response that which we connote as "faith."

Biblical faith requires both a report and a response. The report is God's revelation of what is going to come to pass before it actually comes to pass. Now, having received God's report, the hearer responds according to what God has reported. Where revelation and response touch, faith occurs! Should individuals fail to respond to God's report, they act faithlessly. Should they respond before God reports, they are presumptuous. Both faithlessness and presumption are sin.

Sometimes we are so certain of God's will when He has yet to reveal it. We engage in so many activities assuming (presuming) that we know His full intent. We launch out, "knowing" against all odds, that what we're doing is without a doubt the right thing to do. Then, when our venture fails, we become distraught and discouraged and often seek to blame God for not holding up His end of things.

▪ THE HOLY SPIRIT AND PRAYER ▪

Some of the best-intentioned persons have experienced failure because they misunderstood what God's Word, the Bible, had to say on a matter. Venturing forth toward failure based upon their own interpretation rather than on God's, they then turn to accuse God's Word of error or God Himself of spiritual default. But the problem is ours, not God's. And indictments of the Lord produce no alleviation of failure; rather, they compound the sin.

Since sin is our problem, we need to confess it to Him. But, the Holy Spirit Himself initiates the very confession that is ours. How? Read on...

ALIVE IN THE SPIRIT

8

CONFESSION OF SIN

Although there is no observable correlation between the earliest New Testament book (the epistle of James, A.D. 45) and the epistle's admonition of confession, it is interesting to note that the concept of "confession" spans a half-century, and encompasses the entire timeframe in which the New Testament was written.

"Confession" translates "You all keep on admitting [your] sins to the Lord." Essentially, "to confess" is "to agree with what the Lord has through His Word and by His Holy Spirit declared you to be and to have done." It now becomes apparent why the Lord inspired James to write about confession so early in the Christian era. And our need to "keep on confessing" has not come to termination.

Three appropriate riders attend the Christian confessional. First, confession should be prompt. Paul instructed the Ephesian believers not to sin in their anger; yet, knowing realistically that they would at times become angry, he wrote, "...do not let the sun go down on your anger" (Ephesians 4:26). In other words, if they could not sufficiently submit themselves to the Holy Spirit's control so as to avoid anger, the very least they were to do was to get the matter settled before sundown. Learning as we are today about stress, we may well applaud the Apostle's directive, while remembering that it had a primarily spiritual rather than physical or emotional motivation.

Second, confession should be proportional. Dr. J. Edwin Orr is credited with having said, "Let the circle of confession equal the circle of offense." It has been years since I have witnessed one of the old public confession meetings. In the light of James' directive, we need to "keep on confessing." Still, every asset has its liability. And the public confession meetings are no exception. Some of the things confessed needed to be made right — but with the one who had been offended, not with everyone!

Suppose, for example, in the moments prior to a worship service, you and I engaged in a serious disagreement, resulting in the expression of strong and hateful words toward one another. Neither of us can hope to lead others in worship with factional differences between us. We need to confess our sin.

The record of King David's confession in Psalm 51 convinces us that ultimately all sin is first and foremost against the Lord God. Our anger, therefore, was focused against God before it was ever expressed against each other. So, before either of us can get right with each other (much less, lead a worship service!), we must procure forgiveness from God.

Forgiveness for all sin for all time has been divinely appropriated once for all in the shed blood of Jesus Christ on the cross. But, His blood must be periodically applied to those specific sins of which we are continually guilty. John says as much when he writes,

✠ CONFESSION OF SIN ✠

...and the blood of Jesus His Son continually cleanses us from every unrighteous deed (I John 1:7, Gk. tr.).

For either of us to rise up in the meeting and apprise the congregation of our verbal altercation by allegedly confessing wrong against the other is unthinkable! Apply the dictum: "Let the circle of confession equal the circle of offense." Who was spiritually offended by our actions? The Lord and the other person were offended. First, I must confess to the Lord my wrong — despite the fact that I believe you to be more wrong than I! When I have expressed agreement with what the Lord's Word says about me and about my sin; and about what the Holy Spirit has made me understand through His indwelling presence; and asked forgiveness from the Lord, He applies the blood He shed 2,000 years ago to my sin and forgives me as stated in I John 1:9:

If we are confessing our sins, He is faithful and just in order that He might forgive for us our sins and to cleanse us from every unrighteous deed (Gk. tr.).

Now, I have need only to share with you that the Lord has forgiven me and to ask that you, too, forgive me for what I said and the angry manner in which I expressed myself. When it is over, it is over! We are not devious because we have chosen not to reveal something that could only result in hindering someone's spiritual walk with Christ.

In the same vein of thought, I cannot publicly criticize someone and then privately apologize. If I have committed the wrong in public, it is before that same public that I should make amends. "Let the circle of confession equal the circle of offense."

If the sin is one of mental fantasy, it should be confessed only to God. He alone knows your mind and heart. The sin is there as a thought and must be confessed; but it must be confessed only unto God. To "confess" mental-attitude sins before others is only to implant in their minds the garbage you are acknowledging to be sinful. Again, "Let the circle of confession equal the circle of offense."

Third, confession should result in praise! We all know how good we "feel" when we have amended a wrong. Sin indeed grieves the Holy Spirit. When He is upset, we know that upset within us. Thus, when the wrong has been set right with God and with any others whom we may have wronged, we should experience the need to exalt and praise the Lord! After all, who can forgive sin but God? And He did forgive and He continues to forgive. Surely there is no greater reason or occasion for rejoicing in Him!

But, suppose you experience all of this toward God, but find the offended, human party unwilling to forgive you? Is that an occasion to rejoice? Perhaps not, in the sense that your rejoicing would be more effulgent if forgiveness were extended. Still, you have been forgiven by the One against Whom you most seriously sinned. And you have presumably done everything humanly possible to right the wrong against your fellowman. The bottom line is this: if the offended fail or refuse to forgive you, that is his problem — not yours. It would only be yours if you had made no effort to gain forgiveness or had made some quasi-effort that could easily be distinguished as phony. Only then, do you continue to have a problem. Just forget it. Remember that Paul said to Timothy,

> *Reject a factious man after a first and second warning, knowing that such a man is perverted and is sinning, being self-condemned* (Titus 3:10-11).

The Holy Spirit works out through believers in an effort to produce within them precisely what the Father desires.

▪ CONFESSION OF SIN ▪

All of the Spirit's indwelling is unto this end: that He might reproduce the life of Jesus Christ in the life of the human believer.

What the Holy Spirit actually produces in the believer's life is spiritual fruit. Paul identifies this fruit in his Epistle to the Galatians:

> *But the fruit of the Spirit is love, joy, peace, longsuffering, gentleness, goodness, faith, meekness, and temperance...* (Galatians 5:22-23, KJV).

Unfortunately, the assignment by some of their own meaning to the "fruit" in this passage has obscured the view of many believers to the writer's true meaning. It is important that we clearly and consistently interpret the nature of the "fruit" mentioned here alongside other passages that discuss spiritual fruit. It is poor and unacceptable interpretation to arbitrarily call the "fruit" in John 15 one thing and the "fruit" in Galatians, chapter five another.

Some, for instance, would insist that the "fruit" mentioned in John 15:8 refers to those whom believers have seen converted to Christ under their witness. Our Lord's words, "Herein is My Father glorified, that ye bear much fruit...," would certainly seem to weigh heavily on the side of bringing lost souls under His glorious salvation. And indeed, He is glorified through the salvation of souls. It is precisely through the salvation of souls that He vindicates Himself against Satan's conclusion that He has lost the eternal warfare. Yet, we must be careful not to allow our theological view — however correct it may be — to dictate Scriptural interpretation. Theology derives from interpretation; not interpretation from theology.

One might ask, in the light of John 15:8, whether the Father was "glorified" in the life of Adoniram Judson, who spent 14 years ministering in Burma before he saw his first convert to Christ. Or whether Dr. David Livingstone was "bearing fruit" for those seven years he served in Africa before he witnessed his first convert. If "fruit" must be interpreted as "souls," then neither man was "fruitful" until converts were won. Logically then, neither man glorified the Lord for most of his missionary life and service. Such an understanding is totally foreign to everything else we know about God, empirical arguments notwithstanding.

Dr. G. Campbell Morgan identifies the fruit in Galatians 5:22-23 in correlation with the attributes of Christ's life. Morgan cites *love* as the essential attribute underlying each of the others. *Joy* is identified as "the consciousness of love"; *peace,* as "the confidence of love"; *longsuffering,* as "the habit of love"; *gentleness,* as "the activity of love"; *goodness* as "the quality of love";[1] *faith* as "the quantity of love"; *meekness* as "the tone of love"; and temperance as "the victory of love."1 What a life to know and live — if only we were yielded to the Spirit's control!

Furthermore, it is both reasonable and consistent to interpret "fruit" from John 15:8 in the same way. The Holy Spirit works to reproduce these attributes of Christ in the believer's life.

Be careful to note that it is the "fruit" of the Spirit, not the "fruits." It is *singular,* not plural. This emphasis came to me most graphically some years ago when I was engaged in itinerant evangelism in Australia. One evening after services, my host asked if I would like to taste a "monstereo delicio." I had no idea what a "monstereo delicio" was, but quipped that I would try anything once as long as it was non-alcoholic!

---

1 G. Campbell Morgan, *The Westminster Pulpit* (London: Pickering and Inglis, Ltd., n.d.), 171-179.

▰ CONFESSION OF SIN ▰

He assured me that I could taste some thirteen kinds of fruit in this one tropical fruit. I could hardly wait! To be truthful, I could not taste thirteen kinds; but I did taste several: apple, banana, grape, cherry, pineapple — I could hardly believe it! Additionally, there were different textures as well. What I also discovered was that I could not enjoy the apple without the banana; nor could I have the grape without the pineapple. It was all or nothing!

So it is with the "fruit" of the Spirit. You cannot have peace without being long-suffering. You cannot have joy unless you are also gentle and good. You cannot separate the "fruit" of the Spirit, the attributes of Christ.

In an ingenious way, the Holy Spirit has provided means whereby we may express the attributes of Christ. He provides us certain "gifts," the use of which enables us to benefit the Church in practical ways.

What these gifts actually are, and how they benefit the church is discussed throughout the next three chapters.

ALIVE IN THE SPIRIT

9

GIFTS OF THE SPIRIT:
THE *SERVING* GIFTS

The Holy Spirit is indeed the supreme gift of the Father to the believer. At the same time, the Spirit Himself gives gifts to the believer. Every believer receives at least one gift from the Spirit.

> *But one and the same Spirit works all these things, distributing to each one individually just as He wills* (I Corinthians 12:11).

All believers, therefore, are responsible to know and develop the gift or gifts they possess. Paul admonishes us as he did Timothy to "kindle afresh the gift of God which is in you" (II Timothy 1:6).

Paché defines "spiritual gift" as a

> ...certain qualification given by the Spirit to each individual believer to enable him to serve within the framework of the body of Christ.[1]

---

1 René Pasché, *The Person and Work of the Holy Spirit* (Chicago: Moody Bible Institute, 1966, 180).

Chafer says essentially the same thing, except that his emphasis is perhaps a bit more upon the Spirit's doing. He says that

> ...a gift in the spiritual sense means the Holy Spirit doing a particular service through the believer and using the believer to do it.[2]

That the spiritual gift is to be viewed as different from a natural gift needs hardly to be said. Natural gifts are talents, and may certainly be utilized by the Holy Spirit in the service of the Lord. Spiritual gifts, however, are infinitely more than a mere heightening of natural abilities. A natural gift may or may not be used for the Lord; a spiritual gift must always be in the Lord's service.

What is more, the spiritual gift must always operate within the framework of the local church. Spiritual gifts are never functional outside of their scriptural delineation.

> *But to each one is given the manifestation of the Spirit FOR THE COMMON GOOD (I Corinthians 12:7, emphasis added).*

Again Dr. Draper admonishes the Church to recognize the Holy Spirit's place with respect to spiritual gifts.

> The administering of the gifts, the directing of the body of Christ, is the work of the Holy Spirit. What we have to do is get back to what God has assigned us to do. There is a grand diversity of gifts administered by the Holy Spirit. If we will do it God's way, the world will be absolutely amazed at what happens through His people.... The task of

---

2 Lewis Sperry Chafer, *Systematic Theology, in locus,* Vol. 6, p. 216.

⁍ GIFTS OF THE SPIRIT: THE SERVING GIFTS ⁌

our churches is to agree with the Holy Spirit.[3]

I can only add my "Amen," and note that God's will is for His people to be humble in the recognition of the gifts He has given them. No believer, therefore, is to gloat over his own spiritual gift; nor is he to belittle the gift another possesses. Spiritual gifts are never inconsistent with love or with wisdom (cf. I Corinthians 12:31-13:1).

Nor is any spiritual gift ever out of balance with any other spiritual gift. If that were true, the body of Christ could hardly experience anything but schism. The functional manifestation of the true, spiritual gift is never divisive (cf. I Corinthians 12:25).

Although the Bible offers several lists of spiritual gifts, they may easily be organized into the following three categories: *Serving* gifts, *Speaking* gifts and *Sign* gifts.[4]

Of the seven serving gifts, **FAITH** is the enabling gift, allowing the possessor to look through immediate difficulties and discern the Lord's sufficiency for the situation. Paul possessed this spiritual gift, as we note from his experience en route to Rome.

> *...I urge you to keep up your courage... For this very night an angel of the God to whom I belong and whom I serve stood before me, saying, "Do not be afraid, Paul; you must stand before Caesar..."* (Acts 27:22-24).

---

3 Draper, *Foundations of Biblical Faith*, 31.

4 Attribution of these categories and the general definitions goes to Earl D. Radmacher, Th.D., Chancellor, Western Baptist Theological Seminary, Portland, Oregon.

▪ ALIVE IN THE SPIRIT ▪

Here the indwelling Spirit of God enables Paul to look beyond his immediate peril and to know that the same Lord who has been adequate for every need in the past will now be adequate to control this situation.

Do you not know people who seem to "have it altogether" even when circumstances seem beyond solution? Sure you do. And we often credit their "having it altogether" as part of an easy-going personality. In some instances, that may be true; but in others it is the operation of the gift of faith in their spiritual life.

DISCERNMENT of SPIRITS affords protection to the church. Discernment is the ability to tell a false spirit from the true Spirit of God. Nowhere is this more dramatically apparent than in the experience of Peter with Ananias.

> But Peter said, "Ananias, why has Satan filled your heart to lie to the Holy Spirit...? (Acts 5:3)

Nothing could account for Peter's knowledge of Satan's working in Ananias other than that the Spirit had so gifted him. Nor could anything else account for his perception that Simon the Sorcerer had been caught up in "the bondage of iniquity" (cf. Acts 8:23).

Somewhere I read an account of D. L. Moody that convinced me he possessed the gift of discernment. It was during one of his meetings that he pointed out a particular man and asked a companion who the man was. The companion replied that he was just one of the ushers.

"Get rid of him," was Moody's unexpected instruction. "I don't like the looks of him." According to the account, the man Moody singled out later assassinated President Garfield.

⬛ GIFTS OF THE SPIRIT: THE SERVING GIFTS ⬛

Sometimes we view this spiritual gift as heightened human perception. We must be careful not to incorrectly assign those gifts the Lord intends us to understand spiritually. Surely, to misread the gift of discernment is to acknowledge not possessing it!

HELPS is the spiritual ability to do whatever needs to be done in accordance with the natural ability one has. In other words, the Spirit initiates the desire to do within the body of Christ whatever one is enabled otherwise to do. Paul urges the Roman Christians to help Phoebe "in whatever matter she may have need of you" (Romans 16:2).

One of the young women in our church noticed that the library books were not as accessible to the members as they should have been. She asked about moving the books into another location where they would be more amenable to the congregation. That is an exercise of the gift of helps.

Some people are not gifted to organize others into a working unit, but they are gifted to work within the unit. Such is the gift of helps.

MERCY is possessing the heart to perform merciful deeds toward those who have a genuine need for them. Paul cited for mercy the one whom he ordered disciplined in Corinth, apparently leaving the responsibility for comfort open to those who possessed the spiritual gift.

> *Yet we do speak wisdom among those who are mature; a wisdom, however, not of this age, nor of the rulers of this age, who are passing away* (I Corinthians 2:6).

ALIVE IN THE SPIRIT

On other occasions he cited men like Timothy and Tychicus as possessing this gift. Of Timothy, Paul wrote,

> ...and we sent Timothy, our brother and God's fellow worker in the gospel of Christ, to strengthen and encourage you as to your faith (I Thessalonians 3:2).

And of Tychicus, he stated,

> And I have sent him to you for this very purpose, so that you may know about us, and that he may comfort your hearts (Ephesians 6:22).

The word "mercy" means "taking the hurt out." Over many past years, I have stood beside many sorrowing believers during their hours of bereavement. I have prayed, read Scriptures of comfort and resorted to human reason *(He's so much better off than we are.)*. But when one who has previously experienced like sorrow comes forward, puts their arm around the bereaving spouse and says, "Mary, I lost Tom just a year ago. It'll be all right. The Lord will enable you to survive," I must confess that it is most effective. And why not? It is the utilization of the gift of mercy, working through one believer unto another.

MANAGEMENT (also designated Administration) is the ability to efficiently manage the work of the Lord. Although the context relates to another subject, Paul urges the Corinthian Christians to "let all things be done properly and in an orderly manner" (I Corinthians 14:40).

Let's face it: Felda was a terrible cook. One would be hard-pressed to imagine a more bland and tasteless meal than what she could prepare. But, she was an absolute whiz at organizing cooks for the church kitchen! Felda had no talent for cooking;

■ GIFTS OF THE SPIRIT: THE SERVING GIFTS ■

but she did possess the spiritual gift of management.

LEADERSHIP connotes the ability to mobilize God's people for efficient and smooth action. It is precisely this that Paul has in mind when he instructs Timothy:

> *I solemnly charge you... to maintain these principles without bias, doing nothing in a spirit of partiality* (I Timothy 5:21).

It is doubtful if there is a more spectacular and less enviable serving gift than that of leadership. Management is indeed involved, but a true leader must be what he encourages others to become.

I shall never forget a Christian film that circulated among the churches in the early-to-mid 1960s. One scene was that of a communist leader standing on the courthouse steps personally handing out literature to whomever would receive it. Communist or not, that is leadership! Too many of us as leaders today want to lead from behind the scenes. The very word *lead* indicates *being in front* of the action.

GIVING is the Spirit's enablement of the believer to multiply the material resources he has from God with such efficiency that the work of the Lord is extended. The paramount citation of New Testament giving is that of the Macedonians in II Corinthians 8. They were in "deep poverty," but "begged... for the favor of participation in the support of the saints" (vv. 2-4). Epaphroditus, too, possessed this gift, "risking his life" in order to make up for a financial deficiency on the part

▪ ALIVE IN THE SPIRIT ▪

of the Philippians toward the Apostle Paul.[5]

Brief visitations in Christian homes reveal how much we spend on ourselves! There is no lack of money to do God's work — at home or around the world. The problem is getting those believers who have resources to let go of them as if they were not their own. For in actuality, it is not. The Old Testament teaches tithing; the New Testament teaches that it *all* belongs to Christ from whom it came.[6]

A dear friend of mine over many years founded and led the missionary organization DRIVE in St. Petersburg, Fl. Once each year the organization held a banquet to share with multiple contributors exactly what the Lord had done over the past year and what the vision was for the future. One year, I was asked to be the keynote speaker. And on that occasion, the vision the Lord led the leader to express was underwritten in full that same night by a wealthy, Christian businessman.

When Dr. Harold Fickett was pastor of First Baptist Church in Van Nys, California, I heard him say that if the entire membership were to go on welfare and each commenced to tithe, the church budget would *triple!* The spiritual gift of giving may not always be visible as it is at times, but it always requires accountability.

There is yet more to be said about spiritual gifts. Some are more demonstrative than others. Let's look at what some have called the more spectacular.

---

5 See Philippians 2:30.

6 "Under grace, benevolence will function 'not of necessity' or because of any law requirement; rather does the Christian make his contribution 'as he pruposeth in his heart' (II Cor. 9:7) and 'as God hath prospered' (I Cor 16:2). ~ Chafer, Systematic Theology, Vol. 7, p. 304.

10

GIFTS OF THE SPIRIT:
THE *SPEAKING* GIFTS

Of the five speaking gifts, I believe **PREACHING** is the most prominent. Simply put, preaching is telling forth the Word of God. It is sometimes called prophecy in the sense of forth-telling (as contrasted with fore-telling). When Peter clarified the situation for those confused about the languages spoken at Pentecost, he was preaching.

Men of Judea, and all you who live in Jerusalem, let this be known to you, and give heed to my words (Acts 2:14).

When Stephen held history before the members of the Synagogue of the freedmen (Acts 6:8–7:53), he was preaching. When Paul journeyed from synagogue to synagogue declaring that Jesus was the Messiah of the Jewish people, he was preaching.

A prominent psychologist left his lucrative counseling practice to minister from the platform. He remarked on one occasion that preachers often came to him asking how they could get into counseling. His reply was that God had ordained preaching and that it was the best method ever for counseling people.

For myself, I have learned that preaching has some decided advantages. When you are one-on-one with someone, they have opportunity to argue with your counsel. Convention dictates that they keep quiet while you are preaching. In this way, the minister and the Lord achieve greater effectiveness in counsel.

TEACHING is content-oriented and clearly sets forth doctrine in an orderly manner so as to stabilize believers in the faith. Paul does this most effectively throughout all of his writings. In his Second Epistle to Timothy, Paul gives his understanding of the multiple call he has from the Lord.

> *...for which I was appointed a preacher* (khrux) *and an apostle* (apostoloj) *and a teacher* (didaskaloj) (II Timothy 1:11).

There are many methods of teaching, as witnessed in Jewish rabbis and the Greek philosophers. All good preaching contains teaching; and all good teaching has elements of preaching. One should be careful not to describe these gifts with artificiality. I have heard folks say of a not-too-enthusiastic pulpiteer, "He's more of a teacher than a preacher." Such comments reveal more about the commentator than about the minister of whom he speaks.

One thing is certain to me: were we to select Sunday School teachers on the basis of the spiritual gift of teaching rather than on the basis of sheer availability, we would produce more stalwart disciples for Jesus Christ.

■ GIFTS OF THE SPIRIT: THE SPEAKING GIFTS ■

EXHORTATION may be the most misunderstood of the speaking gifts. Person-oriented exhortation is being able to move alongside someone and help them in a time of need. It is being a counselor, giving forth the Word of God in a spirit of love so as to enable the one in immediate difficulty to move past the difficulty and grow in the Lord Jesus Christ. Paul possessed this gift also, as he states for us in I Thessalonians 2:3, the gift's correct usage,

> *For our exhortation does not come from error or impurity or by way of deceit....*

At the same time, Paul perceives the gift of exhortation in his protégé, Timothy:

> *Until I come, give attention to the public reading of scripture, to exhortation and teaching* (I Timothy 4:13).

KNOWLEDGE is patient study, along with organization and systematization of things of the Lord for use by others in the Lord's work. This is not to say that only those with the gift of knowledge possess any knowledge concerning God's Word; it is rather that those with this gift possess the patience to set it forth in a manner and method that will benefit others.

> *For who has known the mind of the Lord, that he should instruct Him? But we have the mind of Christ* (I Corinthians 2:16).

In one sense, the plethora of study Bibles we have available today is testimony to this spiritual gift of knowledge. They all have things in common; yet, they each have distinguishing features. Each major personality behind each publication has something unique to present. These demonstrate the exercise of the spiritual gift of knowledge.

WISDOM is that insightfulness that, when coupled with practicality, applies the knowledge to a practical end. It is this wisdom that Peter saw in Paul.

> *...and regard the patience of our Lord to be salvation; just as also our beloved brother Paul, according to the wisdom given him, wrote to you...* (II Peter 3:15).

Outside the realm of the Christian faith, we would call this wisdom "common sense." Yet, because the gift is spiritual, it is more than common sense. It is sanctified sense from God.

My wife possesses this spiritual gift. On more than one occasion in our life together, she has expressed genuine wisdom that could only have come from the Lord. I ought only to add (though somewhat reluctantly at times) that on most occasions she was right.

Wisdom is the one spiritual gift for which we may make request. James teaches thus:

> *But if any of you lacks wisdom, let him ask of God, who gives to all men generously and without reproach, and it will be given to him* (James 1:5).

James uses the word σοφία, which means "insight into the nature of a thing." It is Spirit-induced perception. And man can take no credit for such insight.

The usage of certain spiritual gifts has become quite controversial. In the next chapter, we shall examine these gifts.

11

GIFTS OF THE SPIRIT:
The *Sign* Gifts

Sign gifts have always given us more difficulty in understanding. Perhaps it is because they are more controversial in nature than either the serving or speaking gifts. What is important to remember is that sign gifts were given primarily, if not exclusively, to Israel that they might acknowledge the Lord Jesus as their promised Messiah and respond to His teachings.

HEALING is the gift of divine grace to the individual suffering affliction, with a temporal view toward the afflicted person, but ever with a view toward bringing glory to the Lord Himself.

With regard to healing in Scripture, some was more gradual in fulfillment. In the instance of the blind man brought to Jesus at Bethsaida, Jesus spat on the man's eyes and laid hands upon him. But, when He asked, "Do you see anything?" the man replied, "I see men, for I am seeing them like trees, walking about." After Jesus had laid hands upon the man a second time, "he looked intently and was restored, and began to see everything clearly."[1]

So many difficulties surround those who claim the gift of healing today, that the subject of healing has polarized the Christian community into two camps: those who believe that some are still gifted to heal, and those who believe that healing ceased with the end of the first century. Quite candidly, the difficulty is more fundamental still. If we allow that healing as it operated in Jesus' days here on earth is operative today, must we also allow the same for miracles, tongues, or interpretations? And, if we do not allow that healing to operate today, how do we account for the apparently supernatural occurrences that reach beyond the knowledge of present medical science?

The question is obviously not whether the Lord Jesus *can heal* today; it is rather whether He *does so* for the same purpose that He did in the first century, for the Lord is only limited by those principles He Himself established. He is capable of performing anything that does not compromise either His character or His revealed Word. At the same time, I am studiedly persuaded to the contrary of many of the teachings and practices of the modern charismatic movement.

Some years ago in India, a troubled mother beckoned to our small party of four to come aside. We did so, only to understand from our Indian interpreters that she wanted me to pray for her sick child. I had never in my life hesitated to pray for the sick. But, this woman wanted me to lay hands on her child while I prayed. Although I was aware that Jesus laid hands on the sick, I was also aware that Jesus' perception of

---

[1] See Mark 8:23-25.

⁕ GIFTS OF THE SPIRIT: THE SIGN GIFTS ⁕

how and why they were sick was infinitely superior to mine.[2]

I acknowledged that I would pray for the child (although no child was yet visible to any of us), but sought to ignore the request to lay hands on the child. After all, how does one lay hands on someone who is not present? But, the woman kept insisting that hands be laid on the child. Reluctantly, I agreed, while simultaneously inquiring where the child was.

The woman hastened into her humble house and produced the child. My heart sickened at the sight of the child! It was hydrocephalic with the characteristically enlarged head. I made no pretense of being medically knowledgeable (to say nothing of not being a faith healer!), but I knew from previous experience that the prognosis for such a child was not good.

I prayed *within* my prayer that day. The words I openly articulated were underscored with an equally earnest prayer that I might believe to receive what I sought faithfully to ask. The mother was satisfied, never knowing my inward turmoil. We graciously bade her goodbye and there was no further discussion of the incident during my travels in India.

Months later, I received a letter from my Indian friend who had acted as my chief interpreter. At the conclusion of his letter, he added, as if with sudden mental registration, "By the way, do you remember that woman for whose child you prayed? She is ecstatic! For the child has shown marked improvement from that time onward!"

Faith *healing,* yes; faith *healers,* no! Nevertheless, however the Lord chooses to utilize healing, it must ever and always be to His glory!

---

2 In I Corinthians 11, Paul distinguishes the nature of illnesses. The word asqeneij, weak, is used of spiritual weakness (cf. Luke 13:11), while the word ἄρρωστοι (arrhostoi), sick, indicates physical weakness.

■ ALIVE IN THE SPIRIT ■

The gift of **MIRACLES** is much like the gift of healing. The miracles of the Old and New Testaments served to glorify the Lord. Jesus' miracles seemed primarily to focus upon Him as the Son of God. In the final analysis, His message, not His miracles were the most important.

By definition, miracles are God's beneficent, active intrusion into the affairs of humankind that reach beyond human ability. Their purpose is to bring attention to the message and the Messenger as being from God the Father.

Bob was an American friend whom I met in Australia. He and his family had ministered to Aborigines in Western Australia. But, times that were hard became harder still. The family food supply ran out completely, and the situation quickly turned critical. Of course, they prayed.

Back in Queensland, a faithful servant of the Lord was moved in his heart to send £50.00 (at the time, about US$112.00) "to a missionary named *Bob*." His only problem was that he knew no missionary named Bob. So, he took to the telephone and systematically called every missionary organization in the area, asking if they had a missionary named Bob.

The first mission he found with a missionary by that name, immediately received his 50 pounds! The money was sent immediately to my friend in Western Australia. And it was just in time to spare his family their severest crisis to that date.

My most personal, memorable miracle occurred one night in Florida in an evangelistic crusade. Our venue was a tent, and in Florida that in itself might be termed either faith or foolishness. The inevitable winds blew! And more than once, I seriously feared that the night's meeting might have to be

▪ GIFTS OF THE SPIRIT: THE SIGN GIFTS ▪

cancelled. As I sat on the platform, I awaited my time to preach. It was in my heart that I should publicly ask the Lord to calm the winds and the rain. No, I can't do that, I thought. How ridiculous I will look, asking the Lord to calm the winds. When it doesn't happen, it will lessen the confidence of my audience in the Lord's message. I had it all worked out. But, when I stood to pray just before I preached, I found myself praying, "Lord, still the winds of this storm that your Word may be heard and that You may be glorified in and through this service tonight."

Immediately — and I mean *immediately!* — the winds stopped dead still! I was almost too scared to preach. But, with a miracle right there before me, I would have been scared *not* to preach.

A hospital chaplain once said to me, "Every miracle is of the Lord. It's just that in some instances, He chooses to use doctors; and in others, He chooses to do it by Himself." It has been my blessing to witness both.

No spiritual gift has caused more concern to the Christian Church than the gift of "tongues." What are "unknown tongues?" Does the Spirit really give such a gift? And is this gift operative within the church today?

Let's examine this gift in the next chapter and in the two appendices at the end of the book.

ALIVE IN THE SPIRIT

12

WHAT ABOUT "TONGUES?"

With respect to the sign gift of **TONGUES**, I have researched and written so thoroughly that it seems hardly necessary to reiterate it all here.[1] Let it be sufficient to say that tongues (γλωσσαι) were ever and always a language; and that whatever the language discerned, it was *there to bring the Jewish people to faith in Christ.* Every mention of tongues in the New Testament has Jews present. When they are lost, they are evangelized as prophesied in Isaiah 28:11; when they are saved (as with Peter and his company in Acts 10), tongues served as an authenticating sign during the transitional era between the dispensations of Law and Grace. They served to indicate to Christians that the Gospel had indeed been extended unto the Gentiles.

All thoughts that tongues are some kind of "angelic language" or are only for one's "private devotion with God" are totally without Biblical foundation, the sincerity of some earnest believers notwithstanding. With the completion of the Scripture by at least the end of the first century, everything

---

[1] 1 See *Appendix A* on "Tongues" for a more complete discussion of the subject.

necessary for the evangelization of the Jews was present. It was of this time that Paul had announced that "tongues shall cease of themselves" (γλῶσσαι, παύσονται· εἴτε γνῶσις, καταργηθήσεται) [I Corinthians 13:8].

It logically follows, therefore, that with tongues having ceased their operation by at least the end of the first century, the need for **INTERPRETATION OF TONGUES** also ceased. It should not escape the notice of any well-intentioned believer that the interpretation of anything by its nature is highly subjective. Nor am I oblivious to the fact that such includes the interpretation I am offering in this very context. In the effort to avoid biased subjectivity, we must approach the Scriptures with as fully an open mind as possible for the purpose of determining what the Scriptures themselves have to say.

With respect to all of the spiritual gifts, foremost is the truth that they are given by the Lord to His church *for His glory*. Not one gift exists for the personal benefit of any believer.

Once the Holy Spirit has molded man more in the likeness of Christ, He utilizes him that he might be "to the praise of His glory..." (Ephesians 1:12). It was, in fact, the promise of Christ that when the Holy Spirit would come, He would bear witness of Him (John 15:26). Immediately thereafter, the Lord Jesus stated, "...you will bear witness also..." (John 15:27). The simplest, though hardly comprehensive, interpretation of the promise is that the Holy Spirit would come, revealing Jesus as the promised Messiah), first *to,* then *through,* converted, Spirit-controlled believers.

The baptism of the Spirit, therefore, is the spiritual act whereby the believer is rendered "dead" unto the family of Adam, (wherein the believer was physically born) and made simultaneously "alive" unto the family of Christ (into which

▪ WHAT ABOUT "TONGUES?" ▪

he has been born again). Spirit baptism regards the believer's relationship to Christ.

The word translated "filling" (πληρουσθε) must be viewed with respect to the Spirit's *control* over the believer. Remember, the Holy Spirit is the third person of the Godhead. As a person, it is impossible for one believer to have, say, "half of the Spirit," while another believer has "two-thirds of the Spirit." John the Baptist said, "He gives the Spirit without measure" (John 3:34). The "filling," therefore, is best viewed as His control, and regards the believer's fellowship with Christ.

One of the most delightful examples of the Lord's utilization of human beings is recorded alongside an encounter with His disciples on the shore in the final chapter of John. Times were hard for the disciples. The prophets had promised that an era of peace would accompany the Messiah. They were certain that Jesus was the Messiah; yet the long-awaited Kingdom had not come. What made matters worse was a statement Jesus had made to Pilate saying, "My kingdom is not of this world..." (John 18:36). Had they misunderstood the prophets? Had they misunderstood Jesus? Something was wrong. Maybe they should give it all up. Thus when Peter said, "I'm going fishing," it was natural for them to take refuge in their old way of life. But, it hardly proved to be the same old life, for they fished all night without a catch.

There is little wonder, therefore, how they failed to recognize Jesus on the shore as daylight arrived. He called to them, asking if they had had a good catch during the night. Reluctantly, they answered, "No." But, when He insisted that they cast out their nets one more time — and on the other side! — they did so. To their amazement, so many fish filled their nets that the nets themselves began to break!

⋇ ALIVE IN THE SPIRIT ⋇

The inimitable Dr. Barnhouse once said that the miracle on that occasion lay not in Christ's having directed the fish into their nets, but in His having kept them out of the nets all night long!

So now with the huge catch, they came to land. There stood Jesus, who had kindled a fire and laid on some fish for breakfast. Then comes the delight: He said to them, "Bring some of the fish which you have now caught" (John 21:10). How gracious the Lord is to credit His faithless disciples with something He alone performed!

The Holy Spirit works through the believer. He produces His fruit in the believer's life. He utilizes the believer in accomplishing the divine plan of the Father.

Dr. Reuben A. Torrey wrote,

> Every conversion recorded in the Acts of the Apostles was through human instrumentality; not one, single conversion is recorded there that was not by human instrumentality.[2]

When everything is said and done, the glorification of Christ is uppermost! How can we glorify Christ? Does the Holy Spirit enable us to do this? How the believer glorifies Christ is the emphasis of the next chapter.

---

2 Reuben A. Torrey, *The Holy Spirit* (New York: Fleming H. Revell Company, 1927), 60.

13

GLORIFYING CHRIST!

Finally, the Spirit glorifies Jesus! It was Jesus' firm contention that the coming Holy Spirit, the Comforter and Third Person of the Godhead, would replace Him, the Second Person of the Godhead, and would bring glory and honor to Christ as He had to the Father. "He shall glorify Me...," Jesus said (John 16:14).

Some would no doubt object that by omitting glorification to the Holy Spirit the believer was not giving the Spirit His rightful worship and adoration. To argue in this way, however, flies fully in the face of Scripture. The Scriptures rather suggest that the Holy Spirit does indeed receive due respect when we allow Him to accomplish His primary mission: to bring glory to the Lord Jesus Christ.

How does the Holy Spirit bring glory to Jesus Christ? He glorifies Christ when we yield to His control over our individual lives, and through His Divine construction commence to look and behave more and more like Jesus. What Paul the Apostle wrote to the Colossians was and is true for all believers: namely, "Christ in you, the hope of glory" (Colossians 1:27).

■ ALIVE IN THE SPIRIT ■

The major emphasis of that glory is, of course, focused upon Christ. We are to "be to the praise of His glory" (Ephesians 1:12). But, there is a sense in which Christ "in us" is the hope of glory to others also. For as we yield ourselves to the control of His indwelling Spirit, His ministry through us is realized within others who, like us, are objects of His saving grace.

My family and I spent five wonderful years in Australia. We met some of the finest Christian people we've ever known anywhere in the world. We were blessed by the Lord in being able to touch lives for His glory. Many were saved, and many renewed their commitment to Christ.

One life, however, served as a supreme trophy to God's grace. Alf was married to a fine, Christian lady. They had several lovely children, who attended church quite regularly. But Alf was lost. He treated me with the highest respect, but apparently wanted no part of the Savior I preached.

One night, in a Baptist Church in Green Valley, Alf heard the Gospel. I distinctly remember saying in my message, "I've heard *everything* — everything low, mean and ugly that has ever been done. I'm totally unshockable!"

Experience had failed to teach me that superlatives were not only unnecessary, but quite indefensible. Still, no one challenged my statement or my message.

Some weeks later, my team and I were ministering in a Church in Cabramatta, nearby Green Valley. Before the service started, a man approached me.

"Do you remember me?" he asked.

"I sure do," I said heartily. "You're Alf from Green Valley."

"That's right," he replied. "Do you remember what you said when you were there?"

⁑ GLORIFYING CHRIST! ⁑

I had no immediate recollection of anything specific, but had that sudden feeling that I indeed had said something I ought not to have said.

"What did you have in mind?" I asked somewhat hesitantly.

"Can we talk, — uh, privately?" Alf inquired.

Now my mind coursed like lightning through its channels seeking desperately to recall what I might have said that would now be troubling Alf.

"Remember?" he probed, "You said you were 'unshockable'? Well, I think you had better sit down, because I am going to shock you!"

That was more than forty years ago, and I have never revealed the contents of that conversation. It is sufficient to say that Alf indeed shocked me with some of the most startling admissions of personal sin I have heard to this day! Remembering the ill-learned lesson of the past, I shall henceforth forever avoid saying that I am unshockable; nevertheless, my education leaped light years through that conversation.

Alf was saved during our discussion that night. He had an old beat-up van he drove. And from that day to the day we left Australia to return home, he loaded that van with people and brought them to every meeting of mine that was within his driving distance. He knew those he brought would hear the Gospel and he wanted them to be saved as he had been. Some indeed were. But, when they failed to respond to the invitation, Alf would bring them up to meet me afterwards, and say, "Hey, Gene! This is 'Fred.' He needs to be saved! He is worse than I was!"

I've lost track of Alf now, although I'm often prompted to pray for him and his wife. He was not an intellectual; to my

ALIVE IN THE SPIRIT

knowledge, he had no outstanding talents. But, his life had truly experienced the transformation of Jesus Christ. And so far as I could determine, he was living his life under the Holy Spirit's divine control. Alf had indeed become ***Alive in the Spirit!*** The man and his wife were alive; and both were living "to the praise of His glory!" May the Lord ever grant the same to us!

APPENDIX A

THE TRUTH ABOUT "TONGUES"

Since 40 percent of the references in Scripture pertaining to *tongues* as under discussion in this writing are found in the Old Testament, it seems logical that our search for the truth about tongues should commence there.

The earliest specific reference to language in scripture is the one recorded in Genesis 10:5. There the nations were divided into their lands, "every one according to his language..." At that point in history, the whole Earth spoke the same language (Genesis 11:1). But, a multi-lingual introduction to humanity was soon to come. God introduced languages in order to scatter the populations — breaking up a group bent on evil at Babel.

The predominant usage of "tongue"[1] or "language" in the Old Testament is connected with the nation Israel; therefore, it is imperative to first evaluate the nation with a view to determining how significantly interrelated the nation and the language are.

---

1 *Tongue*, γλωσσα (glossa), describes both a language and an instrument of the physical body.

≫ ALIVE IN THE SPIRIT ≪

THE LORD'S PURPOSE WITH ISRAEL

Any studied concern regarding Israel must include God's purpose with her. For Israel was God's people, issuing forth from Abraham, who himself had been pagan[2] (Genesis 12). Stating it simply, God formed the nation of Israel to be His evangelistic nation to the other nations of the world. Through her the Lord purposed to spiritually subdue unto Himself the nations that had persistently gone astray since Adam. Promised to the evangelistic nation was a coming Messiah.

The Messiah was the Lord — the all-sufficient Redeemer. All non-Israelite peoples who would accept the Lord of the Jewish nation and submit to the Lord's covenant regulations were to immediately come under the protective custody of the Lord and would in time receive redemption through the coming Messiah.

Furthermore, the Lord had designed that this Israelite nation would reflect His glory unto the lost nations of the world.

> *The people whom I formed for Myself,*
> *Will declare My praise* (Isaiah 43:21).

The tragedy of Israel's failure to realize the Lord's purpose is written in her own blood through countless historic persecutions.

It is a pattern of God's dealings with Israel that, failing to respond to His purpose, she be subjected to the same judgments designed for those whose redemption she would not willingly

---

2 Abram came from Ur of the Chaldees, where religion was centered in the worship of a "triad pantheon: *anu* (sky), *enlis* (atmosphere and Earth), and *ea* (waters)" *(The Westminster Dictionary of the Bible, in locus).*

■ THE TRUTH ABOUT "TONGUES" ■

procure.[3] Still, the nation of Israel was duly warned. All of God's warnings carry heavy penalties. Israel was born in hope; no other nation in history ever had greater opportunity. Therefore, her failure was more tragic than others.

ISRAEL'S HEAVY PENALTIES

Two heavy penalties descended upon the Jewish people as a consequence of her sin. One penalty was her deportation into captivities in the divine effort toward discipline. Failing to respond to the Lord's disciplines, Israel was dispersed throughout the nations. The late Dr. Donald Barnhouse said that the miracle of Jonah was not that he was swallowed by a whale and lived; the miracle was rather that he was not digested! For the Jew has never totally lost his identity! We might further suppose that their maintenance of identity is itself a reminding mark of God's sure penalties upon nations who reject His will.

Another penalty heaped upon Israel was one of utter humiliation. Since the intended evangelistic nation refused to evangelize others, God would see that Israel would herself be evangelized by a people with a foreign tongue.

> *Indeed, He will speak to this people*
> *Through stammering lips and a foreign tongue*
> (Isaiah 28:11).

That such an endeavor was indeed humbling to Israel is partially demonstrated in her revival of Hebrew as the Israeli national language. No other people in the history of the world has ever revived its dead, native tongue after 2500 years! And should the skeptic suppose that such a feat was

---

3 See Deuteronomy 28:43-68 and Hosea 8:3, 7-8, 11-14).

initiated solely for purposes of practical communication for varied-languaged peoples migrating to a new country, it is suggested that he visit that Land and view Jewish pride in its new Hebrew tongue!

THE JEWISH DISPERSION

Israel's dispersion cannot be exclusively isolated to either a single timeframe or a single event. Yet, for our focus, the time of Alexander the Great (356-323 B.C.) is singularly important. Alexander's victory at Issos was most decisive. Thereafter, the whole of the Mediterranean became his. Subsequently, he marched against Jerusalem. Dr. A. H. Newman, noted Church historian, remarks that the Jews surrendered quite peacefully to Alexander.

> The leaders of the people made prompt, unconditional, and cordial submission to Alexander the Great in 332 B.C. He was so favorably impressed by their attitude and their representations that he treated them with the utmost consideration. The wide dispersion of the Jews, and their ability to be of service to the conqueror as guides to every part of the East and of Egypt, no doubt had something to do with the cordiality of his bearing.[4]

Something, yes; but not everything. The first-century historian, Josephus (A.D. 37-100), records that Alexander and his soldiers marched against Jerusalem. They intended to plunder the city; but when Alexander saw in the distance the priests dressed in white, he went forward, saluted the priests, and "adored" the name of God, which was engraved upon the breastplate of the high priest. When questioned regarding his peculiar attitude toward the Jews, Alexander replied, ably

---

4 A. H. Newman, *A Manual of Church History,* Vol. I, 39.

■ THE TRUTH ABOUT "TONGUES" ■

relating the details of a dream he had had in Macedonia.

> I did not adore him, but that God who hath honored him with his high priesthood; for I saw this very person in a dream, in this very habit, when I was considering with myself how I might obtain dominion over the Persians; whence it is, that having seen no other in that habit, and now seeing this person in it, and remembering that vision and exhortation which I had in my dream, I believe that I bring this army under the divine conduct, and shall therewith conquer Darius, and destroy the power of the Persians, and that all things will succeed according to what is in my own mind.[5]

Furthermore, Hecateus, a Jew of that time, attests that Jews went with Alexander as auxiliaries; after Alexander's death, they went with his successors. Thus, the Jews, whether captive or conciliatory, were duly dispersed throughout the entire Hellenistic Empire.

REJECTION OF THE MESSIAH

In the fullness of God's time, the Messiah came. God's promises are sure. Nevertheless, Israel had throughout centuries of rebellion against God's supreme purpose for her so multiplied the trivialities of religion and worship, that she failed to understand even the parables the Lord Jesus spoke. Much less did she recognize Him as Savior. Christ's own words denote Israel's rejection.

> *O Jerusalem, Jerusalem, who kills the prophets and stones those who are sent to her! How often I wanted to gather*

---

5 Flavius Josephus, *JOSEPHUS' COMPLETE WORKS*, "Antiquities," (Grand Rapids: Kregel Publications, 1960), II, 8:5.

> your children together, the way a hen gathers her chicks under her wings, and you were unwilling (Matthew 23:37).

It was not that Christ was unwilling; it was that *Israel rejected Him!*

> ...and you are unwilling to come to Me, that you may have life.... . I have come in My Father's name, and you do not receive Me... (John 5:40, 43a).

EXPERIENCE AT PENTECOST

More than ten generations had passed by the time the strategic day of Pentecost arrived.[6] Countless thousands of Jews resided throughout the old Hellenistic Empire. Whether the Jewish audience to Pentecost's unique communication was permanently resident in Jerusalem at that time seems inconsequential. The salient factor is that those who heard of "the wonderful works of God" did affirm that they heard in their native language (Acts 2:8-11). The only understanding in accordance with the context is that those who formed the audience for this unique gospel communication had been born in the countries named in the passage.

Thus God, who controls both times and epochs (Daniel 2:21), had gathered this audience for this message at this hour. And in so doing, He fulfilled the prophetic utterance of Isaiah 28:11:

> So at that time in a barbarous (foreign) language (tongue, dialect) and in speech of a different kind, I will bring into order (subdue) this people.[7]

---

[6] Assessing Pentecost at A.D. 34, and noting Alexander's conquest of the Jews at 332 BC, we assume at least 30 years for a generation.

[7] Author's translation from the Hebrew with Septuagint insertions in parentheses.

⚊ THE TRUTH ABOUT "TONGUES" ⚊

Although it may successfully be affirmed that a significant purpose of tongues throughout the New Testament era was the authentication of the Church's redemptive message,[8] it must be simultaneously admitted that the heavily overriding purpose for such an authentication was the subduing of the renegade nation (I Corinthians 14:21).

TONGUES AT CORINTH

Immediately, "tongues" became identified solely as *languages*.[9] Assertions posited by some concerning a distinction between the "tongues" in Acts and those in Corinthians must be regarded as hopelessly superficial. *Glossa* (γλωσσα) translates either as the "organ of speech" or a "language"; *dialecto* (διαλεχτω) translates as a "discourse," or "a dialect of a certain people"; *phone* (φονη) translates as "sound" (I Corinthians 14:10-11).

Had Paul been lending support to some kind of unintelligible, ecstatic utterances, he would no doubt have used the more appropriate fonh. Besides, whatever this carnal church was doing, *it was wrong!* This is Paul's purpose in writing: he wants to *correct* the misuse of a spiritual gift — not to encourage it.

Involved in this corrective discourse is Paul's attention to the *way* spiritual gifts are dispensed: the Holy Spirit gives what He wills to whom He wills; notwithstanding, God's own decree is that some gifts have a definite time for termination (I Corinthians 13:8).

---

8 B. H. Carroll, *Interpretation of the English Bible*, "James, I & II Thessalonians and I & II Corinthians (Nashville: The Broadman Press, 1942), 220-221.

9 W. E. Vine, *An Expository Dictionary of New Testament Words* (Old Tappan, NJ: Fleming H. Revell Company, 1966), articles on "Tongues" and "Language," *in locus*.

■ ALIVE IN THE SPIRIT ■

Keys to understanding difficult passages in Scripture are often found within the Scriptures themselves. We do violation to the revelation of God when we look *exclusively outside* the Bible for answers to questions raised from within the Bible.

"Tongues" are for a sign (I Corinthians 14:22). Of this there can be no serious question. And they are said to be a sign to the unbeliever. Had Isaiah 28:11 never been written, we might well have supposed "the unbeliever" to be simply all unbelievers. But the presence of this prophecy *plus* the correlative, historic record weigh heavily against ignoring the Jewish nation as of particular interest to God. Nor can the identifying phrase, "this people," be relegated to the world-at-large.

The key here that identifies the Jewish nation as the "unbelievers" is in I Corinthians 1:22, "For indeed Jews ask for signs..."

We may, therefore, assess that "tongues" were the *sign* to the unbelievers, *the Jews,* and in so concluding, do violence to neither the logic of Scripture nor the rules of Biblical interpretation.

Yet, Paul said he was glad he spoke in tongues more than the Corinthians. Paul's spiritual maturity allowed him the *proper usage* of the gift. The immaturity of the Corinthians had been the primary contribution toward their misuse of it (cf. I Corinthians 3:1-4 with I Corinthians 14:18-20). Paul could not at that time forbid the usage of the gift (although he forbids *misusage* of it!), because the point of termination for that gift had not yet come. That it did indeed come shall presently be demonstrated.

It should also be noted that every specific instance of speaking in tongues in the New Testament is accompanied

■ THE TRUTH ABOUT "TONGUES" ■

by the physical presence of Jews, whether believing or unbelieving. If it be argued that some of the Jews present on those occasions were already believers, and therefore, not in need of evangelization, then the "sign" must be viewed in its *secondary* sense: that is, the authentication of the message of the Church and the descent of the Spirit upon all believers at the moment of their conversion, Jews and Gentiles alike (Galatians 3:28).

Accepting that "tongues" existed solely for the evangelization of the Jewish people in the initial stage of the Christian era, erases the personal edification aspect altogether. Many charismatics today say, "I only speak in tongues privately. It is of personal, spiritual benefit." Such an insistence must be weighed in the balances of true, scriptural emphasis. If the Scriptures do indeed specify that tongues were for Jewish evangelization alone, then our charismatic friends must at this point be found standing in opposition to teaching from God's Holy Word. We must ever allow *only the Word of God* to stand as the norm of Christian belief — *sola Scriptura!*

Paul does seem to chide the immature, Corinthian believers for their selfishness (if not for their arrogance!) in their private use of tongues. He seems to be saying, *You ought to be concerned for the whole Church, not merely for yourselves* (I Corinthians 14:26). Without question, Paul lists prophecy far ahead of tongues! After all, tongues — in an assembly, at least.— need interpretation; and once interpreted, they become prophecy, *preaching!* So, "desire earnestly to prophesy" (I Corinthians 14:39).

THREE TERMINATING GIFTS

Finally, we come to the consideration of the three terminating gifts: prophecy, tongues, and knowledge.

> *Love never fails: but if there are gifts of prophecy, they will be done away; if there are tongues, they will cease; if there is knowledge, it will be done away* (I Corinthians 13:8).

The superiority of love is clearly visible. This is the whole purpose of I Corinthians 13. What we are is infinitely more valuable to God than what we do or what we know. And in the light of love's endurance, those subordinate gifts will disappear.

Prophecy, tongues and knowledge will come to an end. Prophecy is to be dually understood. Initially, we view prophecy as *foretelling.*

> *Behold, a virgin will be with child, and bear a son, and she will call His name Immanuel* (Isaiah 7:14).

Isaiah spoke these words more than 700 years before the birth of the Messiah. He prophesied, or foretold, what would occur. Basically, however, prophecy is *forthtelling.* This is the root meaning, since the declaration is first voiced or written and then acquires futuristic concepts.

> *And Paul stood in the midst of the Areopagus and said, "Men of Athens, I observe that you are very religious in all respects"* (Acts 17:22).

Paul preached at Mars Hill; and *preaching is prophecy.*

Tongues were for the evangelization of the Jews. They were basically singular in their role; authentication of the church's message seems clearly to be a by-product.

Knowledge is also to be dually understood. In one sense, knowledge means *general knowledge about anything.* Following His washing of the disciples' feet, the Lord Jesus said He had given us an example that all believers should

≈ THE TRUTH ABOUT "TONGUES" ≈

follow. Then He added, "If you know these things, you are blessed if you do them" (John 13:17). Knowledge here is general awareness of Jesus' teachings. But knowledge is also the *divinely appointed ability to communicate doctrine not previously committed to writing.*

Having well established the historical reality of Abraham, Paul the Apostle in Galatians 4:22-25 states that Hagar and Sarah (Hagar, the mother of Ishmael; Sarah, the mother of Isaac) were *also* an allegory.[10]

They were, as indicated, historically real. But where did Paul get this "allegorical" information? It is certainly not readily apparent in the context of Genesis 16-21. Subscribing to the Scriptures as the "God-breathed" Word, we must conclude that the great apostle received this information by *special revelation.* God the Holy Spirit revealed to Paul certain truths not yet communicated in written form.

Thus, all three terminating gifts have to do with communication. *Prophecy* concerned communication of coming events. *Tongues* existed for Messianic communication unto Jews. *Knowledge* dealt with the communication of existent truths not heretofore set forth in writing.

On the grammatical side, the verbs denoting the termination of both foretelling prophecy and specially-revealed knowledge are identical. Their form indicates that at some time future to the time of Paul's writing, both gifts would be done away.[11] The voice form of the verb related to "tongues" indicates that

---

10 An allegory is the setting forth of a narrative in symbolic language.

11 Such is the force of the future passive indicative form of the verb καταργέω (katargeo).

"tongues" will really come to an end by *themselves*.[12] They will cease to be because their whole purpose will have been fully realized.

The real issue involved in the controversy surrounding "tongues" is not *whether* they shall cease, but *when*. Paul wrote that all three gifts would terminate when "the perfect comes"; and the force of the middle-voice verb related to "tongues" in I Corinthians 13:8 leads some scholars to believe that "tongues" ceased by themselves long before "the perfect" came. In any event, all honest grammatical theologians must agree that "tongues" were to have ceased at least by the time of the perfect's arrival, if not before.

Thus, the issue further reduces itself to an explanation of what "the perfect" is, and when it was to have come. Some would have us believe that the perfect refers to our Lord Jesus Christ. This is an immediately ennobling concept. When Christ comes, they say, then "tongues" will cease. Others say it is the church, Christ's body. When the Church is perfected, they say (presumably in readiness to meet the Bridegroom), then "tongues" will cease.

Before we focus on what this phrase really means, we need to remember that the Greek language is the most explicit language ever to exist in human history. If one understands the Greek language of the New Testament, it is virtually impossible to misunderstand the writer's meaning; notwithstanding, the reader must be intellectually honest in his pursuits, and Spirit-led in his theological conclusions.

The Greek language classifies nouns as either masculine, feminine or neuter. The phrase "the perfect" (τό τέλιον) in

---

12 The "reflexive middle" voice adds this dimension to the verb παύσονται (pausontai).

⚋ THE TRUTH ABOUT "TONGUES" ⚋

I Corinthians 13:10 is unmistakably *neuter*. It must, therefore, be translated, "when the perfect *thing* comes…" Were this a reference to Christ, (Χρίστος), it would be masculine (i.e., τόν τέλειον); were it a reference to the Church (εκλησία), it would be feminine (τα' τέλειας).

The only logical and grammatically-correct conclusion one can honestly reach in this matter is that "the perfect thing" refers to the Bible (τον βιβλιον). When the Bible was completed, the need for foretelling as prophecy was eliminated. When the Bible was completed, no special revelations of heretofore unwritten doctrine were any longer needed.

And "tongues" were no longer necessary because the Jew could now be reached through the message in the Bible. That the Bible has survived (like the Jew) when men wanted it to die, is itself a living sign to a sign-seeking people.

We conclude, therefore, by stating that evidence indicates "tongues" to have always been some Earthly language, that the purpose of "tongues," (like the law) was only ever toward the Jewish people; and that any such phenomena existent today must fly in the face of the logical clarity of scripture.

Such a concept will not set well with some. But truth, historically, has always encountered opposition. Furthermore, truth has always emerged victoriously. My sincere prayer is that those who have earnestly and honestly sought to know **THE TRUTH ABOUT "TONGUES"** may now lay to rest any turmoil within their souls engendered by emotional and empirical ideology, and here and now yield themselves totally to the balanced, scripturally-consistent control of God the Holy Spirit. For after all is said and done, the supreme proof of the Holy Spirit's control is not whether one *speaks* in "tongues," but whether there is Holy Spirit *control* over the tongue the believer possesses!

ALIVE IN THE SPIRIT

APPENDIX B

HISTORICAL SYNOPSIS OF TONGUES-SPEAKING[1]

"Tongues" were evident among both hetero-Christian and quasi-Christian groups.[2] Among the hetero-Christian groups, perhaps the oldest was the Kingdom of Mari. Mari was an Ammonite state situated on the Euphrates River in Mesopotamia dating back to the 2nd millennium B.C. The Mari practiced glossolalia (incomprehensible speech, sometimes occurring in a trance). The documents from this period reveal that the Mahhu group was actually a group of priests who worked through the medium of ecstatic inspiration to receive and transmit messages from deities. These Mari documents also prove that the people had great concern for the ecstatic, prophetic experience.

The journey of Wen-Amon of Egypt (ca. 1117 B.C.) gives another picture of this ecstatic experience. Wen-Amon had been commissioned to obtain lumber for a ceremonial barge that was to be dedicated to the Egyptian god Amon. When

---

1 The author is indebted to his good friend, the Rev. Dr. James O. Parks, for the historical research of the information in this appendix.

2 Alfred O. Halder, *Associations of Cult Prophets among the Ancient Semites* (Uppsala: Uppsala University Press, 1945), 21.

≈ ALIVE IN THE SPIRIT ≈

Wen-Amon arrived in Byblos, Syria, he was opposed by the local ruler. While trying to carry out his commission, an Egyptian youth who accompanied him was caught up in a state of ecstasy and became the medium through whom the god Amon spoke. The episode in no way seemed strange to Wen-Amon, and the account was viewed as nothing unusual.

Herodotus (484–425 B.C.) recorded in his history that the worshipers of both Osiris and Isis culminated their worship in an ecstatic frenzy and in a babel of tongues.[3]

Among the Arabs there are two different ecstatic personages of unusual power and influence: the Kahim and the Dervish. Both of these groups go back to an antiquity hidden in Near Eastern tribal culture with elements derived from the ancient rites of Persia and Egypt.

The Kahim stands in the center of a long line of ecstatic succession. One of the primary functions is that of healing.

A Kahim priest enters a state of ecstasy, casting himself upon the body of the patient, and mumbles unintelligible words — speaking in tongues.

The Dervish, through recitation of creeds, religious formulae, prayer and other devices, are induced into a state of ecstasy in which there is a striking parallel to glossolalia, for their messages from Allah are often received through no known tongue.[4]

The Oracles of the Delphi Sibyl, centuries before Christ, were

---

[3] James B. Pritchard (ed.), *Ancient Near Eastern Texts* (Princeton, NJ: Princeton University Press, 1950), 25-29.

[4] Lewis Spence (ed.), *An Encyclopedia of Occultism* (New York: University Books, n.d.).

■ HISTORICAL SYNOPSIS OF TONGUES-SPEAKING ■

among the oldest and most honored of all oracles among the Greeks. These oracles were delivered in a language not known, for the priest had to interpret them as they were uttered during a state of ecstatic possession. An identical type of glossolalia is referred to in Virgil's *Aeneid,* covering the period of 70–19 B.C.

In the Dionysian mysteries, the worshipers often reached a state of ecstasy in which the initiates practiced a specialized type of glossolalia. The Dionysian worship can be traced into Greece at least as far back as the 6th century B.C. Many of the Graeco-Roman mystery religions practiced glossolalia before and even into the era of the Christian faith.[5]

History notes the existence of a number of quasi-Christian groups that practiced speaking in "tongues." The first group within the Christian era, yet outside New Testament mention, were the Montanists. Montanism commenced about 150 A.D. Montanus, before his conversion, was a mutilated priest of Cybele, whose cult was known for somnambulistic ecstasies — tongues.

While many Pentecostal scholars have sought to utilize the Montanist movement as proof of a continuation of the *glossolalia* phenomena throughout history, a brief analysis of the movement makes it doubtful that the Pentecostalists will really want to claim the Montanists as their spiritual ancestors.

The Montanists taught that as Paul's writings superseded Moses,' so their own ecstatic utterances superseded the

---

[5] Samuel Angus, *The Mystery Religions* (New York: University Books, 1966), 264. See also Herodotus, *The Persian Wars,* translated by George Rawlinson (New York: The Modern Library, n.d.) and J. B. Bury, *A History of Greece* (New York: Random House, 1913).

ALIVE IN THE SPIRIT

writings of Paul and the other apostles.

Connected with Montanus were two prophetesses, Priscilla and Maximilla, who, incidentally, had left their husbands. Maximilla taught that "after me there is no more prophecy, but only the end of the world."

The Montanists taught that there were three classes of people (the same doctrine as taught by the Gnostics): the hulic, or unregenerated; the psychic, or ordinary Christians; and the pneumatics, or super-Christians. Through this latter class, Pentecostalism and the charismatic movement demonstrate a spiritual kinship with both the Gnostics and the cult of Montanism.

The movement of Montanus sought to bring back the legalism of the Jews, and taught that speaking in tongues was a sure sign of the soon return of Christ to the earth. They even sought to replace the Holy Spirit with their own leader. Quite definitely they taught that the Bible could be added to by their prophecies.

Another historically proven instance of tongue-speaking among the quasi-Christian community occurred within the Convent of Ursulines in Loudun, France in 1633. The numerous nuns who inhabited the convent showed signs of possession, spoke with tongues, and behaved in the most extraordinary and hysterical manner. A holy brother, Surin, was delegated to terminate the whole affair. During Surin's exorcisms, the demons flippantly answered to the name of Asmodeus, and biblical names, including Leviathan and Behemoth.[6]

The next historically recorded group of tongue-speakers was

---

6 The entire account of this occurrence is recorded in *Historie des Diables de Loudun*, published in 1893.

HISTORICAL SYNOPSIS OF TONGUES-SPEAKING

that of the prophets of the Cevennes or the Camisards. Their dated activities extend from 1685 into the 1700s. Witness some of the teachings and practices of this group:

They saw lights in the sky and heard voices singing encouragement to them. The movement was largely comprised of women and children. Tongues were not a sign of a baptism of the Holy Spirit, but were a sure sign of the speedy return of Christ to the earth.

Dr. Emes, one of their leaders who died on December 22, 1707, taught that he would rise from the grave on March 25, 1708. When he failed to rise, Squire Lacy, the new leader, was prompted to write a treatise to explain why Dr. Emes did not rise from the dead.

Emerging from the Camisards were the Shakers, who ultimately migrated to the United States. The Shakers believed in verbal communication with the dead (spiritualism), a practice expressly forbidden in Holy Scripture (cf. Leviticus 19:31; 20:27).

The Shakers also taught that Ann Lee, their guiding prophetess, was the woman of Revelation 12. Additionally, they advocated a female goddess, for they have rewritten the Lord's Model Prayer to say, "Our Father, Mother, God which art in Heaven."

The Jansenists of France were a protest group within the Roman Catholic Church, and they experienced "tongues" in 1731. Nevertheless, the movement died out within a few years.

The Skoptsy group, originating in Russia around 1765, were also a proven tongue-speaking people. Founded by Danilo Filippov, a deserter from the Czarist army, this group taught that the Bible was not a valid book. Only the living book — the Holy Spirit living in an individual soul — was the true word of God. They believed Jesus Christ to have been an ordinary man who became the Christ upon the cross. They embraced no belief in a literal resurrection of the body of Christ, but taught that He was raised in the spirit. What is more, they said that the Christ-spirit is re-resurrected in every generation; and Danilo Filippov, at the time of his life, was believed to be the present, resurrected spirit of Christ. Speaking in tongues was envisioned as the seal of God by the Skoptsies; and castration was the baptism of fire and of the Spirit.

The Catholic Apostolic Church, or Irvingites, existing primarily from the time of Edward Irving (1792–1834), were proven tongue-speakers. Here listed are some of the teachings and practices of this group:

> 1. Mary Campbell, a young woman supposedly near death (yet not bed-ridden), declared herself to be speaking in the language of the Pelew Islands. Interestingly enough, she had chosen a language not easily discreditable. She later taught that this language was an unknown, supernatural language. Ultimately, she confessed that she had called some of her own impressions "the voice of God."

> 2. Robert Baxter, one of the leaders of this group, spoke sentences in French, Latin, Spanish, Italian and other languages he could not identify.

> 3. The spirit that guided this group of tongue-speakers began manifesting that curious ambiguity that is universally characteristic of spiritualism, despite the contention that this was not a spiritist group.

> 4. The spirit told Baxter to go to the Chancellors' Court, and there be inspired to testify; and for that testimony, he would be cast into prison. Baxter spent three hours at the Chancellors' Court and nothing happened. He returned

◾ HISTORICAL SYNOPSIS OF TONGUES-SPEAKING ◾

home in disgust.

5. The spirit told Baxter that he had been chosen to be a new Isaiah, and at the end of forty days miraculous powers would descend upon him. At the end of the forty days, nothing had happened; whereupon, Baxter decided that they had all been speaking by a lying spirit — not by the Spirit of the Lord.

6. Tongue-speaking by this group was viewed as a sure sign of the soon return of Christ. In fact, they also taught and made predictions relative to the time of the Lord's return.

By the 1830s another group arose advocating "tongues." This group is known today as the Mormons. The origin and teachings of the Mormons are so evidently contrary to the origin and teachings of our Lord, that any avowal of speaking in "tongues" by this cultic group can only fall out to the discredit of the practice.

> I spoke to the conference in another tongue, and was followed in the same gift by Brother Zebedee Coltrin, and he by Brother William Smith, after which the Lord poured out His Spirit in a miraculous manner, until all the Elders spake in tongues, and several members, both male and female, exercised the same gift. Great and glorious were the divine manifestations of the Holy Spirit. Praises were sung to God and the Lamb; speaking and praying, all in tongues, occupied the conference until a late hour at night, so rejoiced were we at the return of these long-absent blessings.[7]

There were some out-breakings of *glossolalia* in the revivals in Scotland and Wales at the turn of the 20th century, but enough

---

7 Joseph Smith, *Joseph Smith's Journal*, January 22, 1833.

of the general history of *glossolalia* has been presented to demonstrate that it occurred only occasionally in the history of the Christian era. Even then, the advocacy and practice was confined to groups that were actually peripheral to the Christian faith.

Thus, the practice of *glossolalia* can be said to have been an isolated phenomenon, occurring sporadically throughout history, and under unusual circumstances, arising from the teachings of humanistic theology.

BIBLIOGRAPHY

Aland, Kurt, Matthew Black, Carlo M. Martini, Bruce M. Metzger and Allen Wikgren (eds). *The Greek New Testament,* 2nd ed. Stuttgart, West Germany: United Bible Societies, 1966.

Angus, Samuel. *The Mystery Religions.* New York: University Books, 1966.

Berggren, Walter C. *The Holy Spirit and His Work.* Polk City, IA: Self-published, 1947.

Bounds, E. M. *Power Through Prayer.* Grand Rapids: Zondervan Publishing House, 1965.

Carroll, B. H. *Interpretation of the English Bible,* "James, I & II Thessalonians and I & II Corinthians." Nashville: The Broadman Press, 1942.

Draper, James T., Jr. *Foundations of Biblical Faith.* Nashville: Broadman Press, 1979.

Gordon, A. J. *The Ministry of the Spirit.* Philadelphia: American Baptist Publication Society, 1894.

Greenfield, John. *Power from on High.* Atlantic City, NJ: The World Wide Revival Prayer Movement, 1931.

Griffith-Thomas, W. H. *The Holy Spirit of God.* Grand Rapids: Eerdmans Publishing Company, 1969.

Gromacki, Robert G. *New Testament Survey.* Grand Rapids: Baker Book House, 1974.

Halder, Alfred O. *Associations of Cult Prophets among the Ancient Semites.* Uppsala: Uppsala University Press, 1945.

Hession, Roy. *Be Filled Now.* Fort Washington, PA: Christian Literature Crusade, n.d.

Josephus, Flavius. *Josephus' Complete Works.* Grand Rapids: Kregel Publications, 1960.

Kittel, Rudolph. *Biblia Hebraica.* Stuttgart: Privileg. Wurtt: Bibelanstalt, 1937.

Martin, Gerald. *How to Be Filled with the Holy Spirit.* Seoul, Korea: The Jordan Press, n.d.

McConkey, James H. *The Threefold Secret of the Holy Spirit.* Lincoln, NE: Back to the Bible Publications, 1965.

Morling, G. H. *The Holy Spirit.* Sydney: Self-published, n.d.

Muller, George. *Answers to Prayer.* Chicago: Moody Press, n.d.

Newman, Albert Henry. *A Manual of Church History,* Vol. I. Philadelphia: The American Baptist Publication Society, 1953.

Owens, John. *The Holy Spirit, His Gifts and Power.* Grand Rapids: Kregel Publishing Company, 1985.

Paché, René. *The Person and Work of the Holy Spirit.* Chicago: Moody Bible Institute, 1966.

Philpot, Joseph Charles. *Meditations of the Person, Work and Covenant Office of God the Holy Ghost,* Vol. 2. Harpenden, U. K.: O. G. Pearce, 1976.

Pink, Arthur W. *The Holy Spirit.* Grand Rapids: Baker Book House, 1984.

Pritchard, James B. (ed.). *Ancient Near Eastern Texts.* Princeton, NJ: Princeton University Press, 1950.

Radmacher, Earl D. *What to Expect from the Holy Spirit.* Grand Rapids: Radio Bible Class, 1983.

Ramay, Marion Edgar. *The Holy Spirit in the Life and Work of the Believer.* Shawnee, OK: Oklahoma Baptist University Press, 1950.

Ramm, Bernard. *A Handbook of Contemporary Theology.* Grand Rapids: Wm. B. Eerdmans Publishing House, 1966.

Rice, John R. *The Power of Pentecost or The Fulness of the Spirit.* Wheaton, IL: Sword of the Lord Publishers, 1949.

■ BIBLIOGRAPHY ■

Spence, Lewis (ed.). *An Encyclopedia of Occultism.* New York: University Books, n.d.

Taylor, Jack R. *After the Spirit Comes.* Nashville: Broadman Press, 1974.

Torrey, R. A. *The Holy Spirit.* New York: Fleming H. Revell Company, 1927.

Tregelles, Samuel Prideaux (transl.). *Gesenius' Hebrew and Chaldee Lexicon.* Grand Rapids: Wm. B. Eerdmans Publishing Company, 1957.

Vine, W. E. *Expository Dictionary of New Testament Words.* Old Tappan, NJ: Fleming H. Revell Company, 1966.

Wilson, Thomas H. *The Holy Spirit.* Verona, MO: Self-published, 1911.

Witty, Robert G. *Holy Spirit Power for the Church.* Jacksonville, FL: Pioneer Press, 1966.

GENE L. JEFFRIES has been engaged in Christian ministry for more than 60 years, serving as a pastor, an evangelist, and in college and seminary teaching and administration. He and his family resided for several years in Australia where he conducted church and area-wide evangelistic crusades. He has traveled widely in the Middle East, Far East, and Europe, visiting and teaching on mission fields.

An author and editor of several works, Dr. Jeffries has also been the principal speaker for **THE EVANGELISTIC HOUR,** heard internationally; **ON COURSE!** and **VANTAGE POINT,** both weekly radio programs that reached parts of Arkansas, Missouri and Oklahoma.

Dr. Jeffries has served as Academic Dean of three post-secondary institutions, and as Founder and President of the St. Louis Institute of Biblical Studies, Cambridge Graduate School and Emmanuel College of Christian Studies. He is listed in *Who's Who in Religion, Men of Distinction,* Cambridge, England, and *Who's Who in Executives and Professionals.* He holds a B.A., M.Div. and Th.D. degree. Dr. and Mrs. Jeffries have three grown children and nine grandchildren. They reside in Springdale, Arkansas.

Why me? Why this? Why now?
No Christian is immune to suffering.

"Enduring Your Season of Suffering" provides practical steps to:

- Understand suffering
- Overcome suffering
- Help others who are suffering

Liberty University professors John Thomas and Gary Habermas have combined their wisdom and years of experience to create a book that answers life's most formidable questions about suffering.

"Enduring Your Season of Suffering" is filled with real-life anecdotes, extensive research and sound biblical truths.

"When we attempt to avoid suffering, we risk missing God's purpose for the pain." - **Dr. John Thomas**

Now available for purchase on Amazon.com and BarnesandNoble.com.
Look for the eBook soon!

 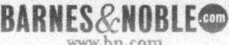

www.ingramcontent.com/pod-product-compliance
Lightning Source LLC
LaVergne TN
LVHW011425080426
835512LV00005B/278